Word
Salad

AND OTHER CHALLENGES OF DEMENTIA

J.E. COOK

DEDICATION

"God never moves without purpose or plan."
- Ron Hamilton

This book is dedicated to all those with a friend or loved one suffering from dementia in any form; and to one in particular, who was a living example of the love of God to those of us who had the privilege of serving on his wife's caregiving team. Daily, he demonstrated a great deal of love and care for his sweetheart during the years we were blessed to assist him with her care.

I count it a privilege to have been among the caregivers for this wonderful lady and I'm honored to be given the liberty to recount in these pages some small portions of that journey for the benefit of others.

One never knows how God might use our personal experiences – good or bad. We need only to trust Him as we walk down each path He leads us to. To quote a favorite song, ". . . my Father knows best, and I trust in His care..."

Thank you, Pastor Tom Rose, for your friendship, and for allowing me to become a part of Marilyn's caregiving team. God used the two of you, even in her illness and death, to teach others of His love and care for His children and what it means to truly sacrifice for others. You were a living illustration of unconditional love.

What a blessing it has been to recount so many memories and lessons of those days.

"Count your blessings, name them one by one, and it will surprise you what the Lord hath done."
- Johnson Oatman Jr.

CONTENTS

LISTS

CHARTS
&
FORMS

ACKNOWLEDGEMENTS

This book would not have been possible without the love and support of my family and friends; and of course, the Lord, Who first laid it on my heart to undertake this work.

I always wanted to be one of those people that God could just whisper in their ear and they'd say, "I hear you Lord; and shall obey post-haste!" Then with immediate understanding and clear direction, they would "rise and go forth," accomplishing astonishing things for God!

Instead - I sometimes forget that life is not, "all about me," which puts me behind the curve in recognizing things I could be doing to help others. Once I figure it out though, you couldn't pull me off it with a crowbar. So - for that, I just want to say, "Thank you God," and thanks for your patience with me.

A grateful thanks also to my daughter, Charity, who spent tireless hours pouring over every page, giving invaluable help and suggestions; and to my son, Quinn, for his faithful assistance and feedback in choosing and tweaking version after version of the cover photo and design; and even to little Mia Claire, who now thinks every salad photo she sees is, "Nonna's book!"

A special thank you to the members of the *Tuesday Night Scripters*, Jan Andersen, Cheryl Chamberlain, April Schave, Dar Streedbeck, and Doug White, who critiqued with diligence and care. Your thoughtful and meticulous efforts in reading and critiquing the work chapter by chapter are so much appreciated.

Thank you also, to those very special friends who sacrificially agreed to be beta readers, and once it was completed, read the book through from beginning to end with objectivity. Each one of you made your own unique contribution and your notes and comments proved very beneficial.

PREFACE

This book came about as a result of my experience on a caregiving team several years ago, which cared for Marilyn Rose, the wife of our associate pastor, Tom Rose. The team was made up of several ladies in our church and we cared for her for eight years, from the time of her initial diagnosis until well into end-stage. Our team coordinator was a nurse working under the supervision of the family doctor and we were able to help her remain in her own home and bypass nursing home care altogether.

The book was finished and left in a drawer unpublished until recently, when a friend was diagnosed with *rapidly progressive dementia.* The news of the diagnosis sent me searching for some of its contents to help put together a caregiving team for her.

It's a pity I left it so long, because my current associate pastor's wife (different church, different lady) was diagnosed with dementia a couple of years ago and her family might have benefited at that time from some of the information in this book. To my shame, I count that as a missed opportunity to have been a blessing to some people I care about.

While reviewing the book for current use, I read through each chapter, reminiscing and reliving many good memories with Mrs. Rose. Because the book was originally part caregiving help/part memoir, a lot of it has been set aside and other parts condensed for this publication. The following pages are the result of that gleaning.

INTRODUCTION

"Please remember the "REAL ME" when I cannot remember you."

- Anonymous

The most difficult day some people may ever face is the day their loved one no longer recognizes them.

Though the subject of this book is not particularly fun to think about, I have tried to keep it on the lighter side, while still providing useful information. I hope it will be helpful in offering you some solutions you can apply to your situation to relieve some stress and lighten your load.

This book was written to caregivers, to give insight into what their loved one with dementia may be experiencing, and to offer support to help them provide the best care possible. It is written mainly for spouses or other family members who are acting as caregivers in the home, and not for professional caregivers. It may also help friends or loved ones not on a caregiving team, who simply want a better understanding of the needs of dementia sufferers. Hopefully it will provide some clarity and confidence for coping with challenging circumstances.

There are probably hundreds of books written about dementia, and just as many differing views on various aspects of the disease. This book is, by no means, an exhaustive resource, but rather a *quick guide to practical advice* on how to deal with various situations at different stages of progression.

The information presented here is gleaned from only the most reputable sources, as well as from eight years of personal experience as a caregiver and ten years of subsequent study. Working with other caregivers, we provided round the clock care for my Associate Pastor's wife, from the initial diagnosis through every stage of progression.

I am not a medical professional. I offer this information solely as advice from a caregiver's perspective, and not as professional medical advice. Some helpful resources are provided in the back of the book for your perusal. A few charts and checklists are included to help organize and execute a caregiving plan for your loved one, should you choose to care for them in the home. Use them as is, or adapt them to your own needs. Permission is hereby granted to reproduce them for personal use. Some of them were taken from other sources and used by permission. For those so notated, permission for use must be obtained from the original source.

For Lynn

J.E. COOK

Dementia Defined

Webster's Dictionary offers a great definition for dementia:

"A usually progressive condition (such as Alzheimer's disease) marked by the development of multiple cognitive deficits (such as memory impairment, aphasia, and the inability to plan and initiate complex behavior)."

According to the Journal of the American Medical Association (JAMA):

"...dementia is diagnosed only when both

memory and another cognitive function are each affected severely enough to interfere with a person's ability to carry out routine daily activities."

This means that a person must have two separate symptoms of impaired brain function in order to be diagnosed with dementia. One is memory loss, and the other may be one of several, such as difficulty with language, impaired judgement, personality changes, or difficulties in social behavior.

Dementia then, is not a disease in and of itself, though often referred to as such, but rather a condition, or syndrome; a group of symptoms resulting from other conditions or diseases. It is a broad term for many sets of conditions involving impairments in thinking, memory and reasoning.

When other conditions exist, such as traumatic brain injury, stroke, depression, and even bladder infections, they can sometimes produce symptoms of dementia. Even taking certain medications under some of these circumstances can cause dementia symptoms to appear. When this is the case, it is often reversible. Treating the condition can reverse the resulting dementia symptoms.

The "go-to" diagnostic standard for mental and psychological disorders (DSM-5) has adopted a new term for dementia: *Major (or Mild) Neurocognitive Disorder*. To destigmatize the disease long considered a mental disorder due to its name, this new term, while more accurate, is currently used primarily by professionals in the medical community. For the average person, the more they learn about dementia, the clearer it becomes that it is a brain dysfunction, rather than a mental disorder as the term suggests.

I Used To Be

If you have someone with dementia in your life, it is important to remember that they are suffering – and the suffering is intense. The patient feels their life crumbling around them. Many people who are now patients, unable to care for themselves in even the most basic ways, were once themselves vital caregiving people. They were parents raising their children. They were the ones who organized events and fundraisers in their communities. They were

Sunday school teachers and daycare workers. They were the "go-to guys," the small business owners, and the CEOs of fortune 500 companies. They were the people who made decisions that affected entire communities.

Now, they need help just feeding themselves or remembering how to get dressed. Some of them may be aware of their loss at times, while others may only remember their own childhoods.

I remember one particular day, when I was helping Mrs. Rose to get dressed. After gathering up one leg of the pantyhose between my thumbs and forefingers I realized that I had done it backward. It would have been correct, had I been going to put them on myself; but since I was putting them on her, they needed to be the other way around. As I tried to wrangle the bunched-up scroll of nylon around to the other direction without them unraveling or getting a run in them, she sat patiently, waiting for me to figure out what I was doing. I finally did, and managed to get them on her up to the knee and then repeat the process with the other leg. The tricky part came when she stood up so I could finish the job. If you've ever put on a pair of pantyhose and then felt like they were *screwed on* instead of *pulled on*, you know exactly what I'm saying. It took a little while but we finally managed to get them all straightened out and then we both plopped down on the bed with a great big "Whewww!" and a good laugh.

There we sat, on the side of the bed next to each other, and both of us happened to look down at our feet at the same time. Neither of our feet reached the floor, and for some reason she thought that was hysterical. We laughed and giggled like two school girls for a couple of minutes; and then suddenly she looked straight into my eyes and said, "Thank you for helping me like this. I hope you never have to have someone help you the way you help me."

Fighting back the tears and trying desperately to regain the light-hearted spirit that had just flown out the window, I replied, "Well, thank YOU, for letting me. It's an honor for me - to be able to help you this way," and I meant exactly that. I admired her determination to hold on to her faculties for as long as she possibly could.

If you are the caregiver for someone you love, please remember that even when it's difficult for you personally, more than likely it's ten times harder for them. Loss of dignity can be very difficult to deal with, especially when they are in stages where they remember some things - sometimes - and at other times they have moments of clarity when the reality of the situation really sets in. <u>Revere</u> those moments of clarity - and use them to communicate with the "*real me*" inside of them. Remember that they will happen less and less frequently, so take those opportunities to REALLY LISTEN to what they are saying to you during those times. It may be vital to their care. It may also be simply a moment when they came to the surface, so to speak, and wanted to spend it with YOU. You may not always know the difference at the time, but that's OK. Just cherish the moment.

Now What?

In the first few weeks or months after a diagnosis, you may find yourself reacting in one (or both) of two ways.

You may be in denial. You may be hoping that the doctors are wrong; or that it will just go away. Your loved one seems fine most of the time. They're strong; they can beat this. You think maybe they're just tired or in need of a vacation.

OR...

You may be hypervigilant. You read everything you can get your hands on about dementia. You watch your loved one day and night, looking for signs of distress, agitation, change, or any other issues that need to be addressed. You're wearing yourself down trying to be available for them. You're drowning in information overload and you aren't sure which "expert" to listen to. It is easy to become frustrated or overwhelmed with differing opinions between doctors, clinics, and researchers about different aspects of the disease, as well as treatments. *That's why I wrote this book.*

Finding a balance between these two reactions is the more sensible approach. There is no need for anyone to be alone on this journey. *It is not a sign of weakness to ask for help.* So as you begin your journey in caring for your loved one, by all means, read all you can about dementia, and then talk to people who understand caregiving. Use as many sources for help and support as you feel comfortable with.

With so much information available, much of it wrought with inconsistencies and controversy, it may be helpful to simply cut through all the loud voices out there promoting this cause or that theory. Just stop – take a moment – and look at what is actually needed to provide your loved one with a safe, happy existence for the remainder of their life.

The purpose of this book is to break down the basics and offer practical, i.e. *applicable* advice, for those who simply want to take care of their loved one, and not get caught up in someone else's cause.

"You're braver than you believe, stronger than you seem, and smarter than you think."
- Christopher Robin (A.A. Milne)

Caregiving Basics

Basic caregiving is just that - basic. A little common sense and a lot of love can get you through many things. However, when you are trying to care for someone with dementia you must remember that you are dealing with someone who has lost, or is in the process of losing, their basic reasoning abilities. Because their reasoning is compromised, they will not always react to things the way they have in the past; so their behavior could become unpredictable. This unpredictability can be very frustrating for caregivers at times, but once you understand that there is no longer any such thing as "normal" in the sense of there being a standard reaction or behavior, you will be able to adapt and be more flexible to roll with the punches.

As I said, I am not a medical expert. I'm not really even a caregiving "expert". I'm just someone who cares about people who cannot care for themselves. I served as a caregiver for several years, and I've done a lot of research on the subject. What I offer you here is what I have learned through experience and study. The things discussed here are things that worked for me and some of the team members I worked with. In most cases, they will probably work for you too; although, since every dementia patient is different, you may have to tweak them to fit your situation.

You can use the following acronym as an easy way to remember the basics of caregiving:

A.L.O.H.A.

Ask, Listen, Observe, Help, Assess

I find it somewhat humorous that the word, "ALOHA" fits so well with basic dementia caregiving instruction. Since the meaning of the word is both, "hello" and "goodbye" I find it funny that it so adequately lays out a plan for how to care for people who are always, "coming and going." Dementia patients are very often stepping in and out of different time frames from their own lives. The caregiver often must enter that "time warp" with their loved one in order to meet their needs. In doing so, they also experience somewhat of a time warp of their own, in the sense of stretching their schedules, re-prioritizing some things in their lives, and sometimes simply making time "stand still" for their loved one when they cannot find their way back to the present.

The Acronym
Ask - **L**isten - **O**bserve - **H**elp - **A**ssess

Ask open ended questions. They have no right or wrong answers and they allow your loved one to use their brain as they try to answer and converse with you. Ask, "How are you feeling today?" instead of, "Are you ok?" Any conversation that lets them speak without feeling they have to come up with the "right" answer will allow them to communicate at their present comfort level.

Listen to what they say, but don't always take it at face value. Reacting, or overreacting, when they say things that seem nonsensical or confusing will only leave you frustrated, or perhaps even angry. There can sometimes be a much deeper meaning behind the words they use. For instance, dementia patients will often say things like, "I want to go home." Do they mean "home" to their house across town? Or do they mean "home" to their childhood home where they grew up and perhaps felt safe and secure, as a child under their parents' guardianship. Ahhh! There you have it. They may actually be saying, "I feel insecure, uncomfortable, or unsafe." Listening "between the lines," and sometimes digging deeper, can often reveal what the actual need of the moment is.

Observe them, and what is going on around them. Watch their body language, their motions, and their moods. People move in a certain way when they have back pain, for instance, or a sore arm or hip. They may sit a certain way that tells you they are physically uncomfortable and need a pillow or some other comfort item. Observing their facial expressions is another good way to determine what their needs are. A facial expression that says, "Yes, I understand what you just said," looks quite different than one that says, "Who are you again? Do I know you?" If you can see by the expression on their face that they are in pain, confused, or agitated then you have identified a need that you may be able to help them with.

Help them with their immediate need (walking, sitting comfortably, eating, taking medication, etc.). Do whatever you can to assist them in finding their own level of comfort. This may take several tries, or several different things to achieve, but helping them feel comfortable, safe, and cared for is the main job of the caregiver at all times. *Our main goal as a caregiver is to, "give care"* i.e., help them be as happy and comfortable as possible.

Assess the situation. Once you've helped

them initially, just watch, and let them tell you with their actions whether the need has been met. They may not always be able to articulate it, but if they are showing signs of agitation or discomfort, this is an indication that there is still a need. Observing them closely is the best way to assess what the real needs are. It may be just a matter of them settling down a bit, or it may be an actual need that went unnoticed.

At times you will want to include in the assessment, an assessment of their language abilities. This can help in the communication of needs. Use the following charts on page 17 to assess language deficits and facilitate communication with your loved one.

Read the charts through ahead of time to remind yourself what you are looking for.

If the information in column 1 applies, use the method in column 2 to improve communication, both in giving (expressive) and receiving (receptive) information.

Perseverance is not a long race;
it is many short races one after the other.
- Walter Elliot

LANGUAGE ASSESSMENT
EXPRESSIVE ABILITIES

IF THEY:	FACILITATE COMMUNICATION BY:
Have difficulty finding the correct word	If you are sure of the word they are trying to say, repeat it. If not sure, don't guess. This increases their confusion and frustration.
Have difficulty creating sentences or a logical flow of ideas	Listen for meaningful words and ideas. Try to identify the key thoughts and ideas. Do not dismiss them as, "totally confused".
Curse, use offensive or aggressive language, or exhibit aggressive or combative behaviors	Don't reprimand. *Respond to the emotion, not the words.* Validate their feelings. Assess for unmet needs, including those related to misperceptions, hunger, thirst, toileting needs, pain, etc.
Avoid verbalization altogether or mutter in various tones that may seem meaningless to others	Read non-verbal communication. Anticipate needs.
Make a choice when presented with two objects or options	Limit choices. Too many options will cause confusion and frustration.

LANGUAGE ASSESSMENT
RECEPTIVE ABILITIES

IF THEY CAN:	FACILITATE COMMUNICATION BY:
Understand a yes/no choice	Ask simple, direct questions that require only a yes or no response.
Read simple instructions	Provide instructions in a place that is easily visible to the patient.
Understand simple verbal instructions	Use short, simple sentences. Use one-step instructions to enhance their ability to process. Example: It's time to get dressed. I will help you (pause and proceed).
Understand instructions given with physical cues	Use gestures. Model the desired behavior (Example: eating). Be sensitive to the fact that, although the person may not understand words, they can read your body language, sincerity, and mood.
Make a choice when presented with two objects or options	Limit choices; too many options will cause confusion and frustration.

Time-Warp

It is important to understand that the dementia patient is suffering from a disease that affects their mind. They have no control over when, where, how, or how often their mind regresses. They do not mean to insult or scare others by their behavior. They are simply responding to circumstances which are beyond their control.

Their lives have become perplexing, as they often do not understand what is happening to them. They may feel confusion or isolation, as their mind fixes on one particular time frame in their lives, and then moves to another, all within a matter of hours or even moments. It's like living in a time-warp from a science fiction movie; jumping from one time frame to another, and then another.

Each day may be brand new for them as they forget familiar places and people. Some are not as deeply affected by this, as they do not know that they do not remember. Others may know it, and become annoyed that they cannot remember. They may feel frustrated at times. They may be alarmed as they become aware they are not thinking or behaving as they used to. Some may notice slowed reaction times or experience a feeling of not being useful.

Paranoia may take over as the patient begins to feel that they are "losing it." These patients may be aware of their caregivers' help and feel that they are losing control. They may feel that the caregiver is "taking over." They may lash out, or even get violent, as their helplessness takes over. Some suffer delusions and hallucinations. Often these are outrageous and easily spotted by the caregiver. Sometimes these "ideas" become so real to the patient that they are convinced of an urgent impact upon their lives.

Mrs. Rose experienced this *paranoia syndrome* several times. The first time was when she thought her husband was next door at the church (he was actually out of town) and that we were keeping him from coming home. She tried to unlock the deadbolt on the front door to go and "rescue" him. He had previously put an extra deadbolt up higher on the door which was veiled by the window curtain and not easily seen. When she couldn't get out, she ran through the house to the back door and tried to go out that way. When that didn't work, she ran back to the front door and turned the knob back and forth, pulling on it repeatedly and yelling, "You're not going to keep me here. I'm going to get Tom and we're getting out of here!" This went on for about 15 minutes, back and forth between doors until finally – she bit me! She literally chomped down on my hand, which was about eye level to her, as I reached up to check whether the deadbolt had been unlocked during all the activity. I must have had a shocked look on my face because the look on hers was that of surprise too. I saw a mixture of, "what just happened?" and something like, "oops I may have gone too far," and then she backed down. Was this a moment of clarity? My guess is yes, but who can say for certain, really?

This was a learning experience for me, being the first of this type of incident with her. When I relayed it to the nurse who oversaw the caregiving team, she said it was an indication that she had now passed into another stage of the disease. That was a sad day for me, as both friend and caregiver, not because of getting bitten, but because it was heartbreaking to see that she was slipping further away from us. Looking back now I think it's possible that when I reached up toward the deadbolt she may have perceived that as some type of threatening gesture. If that were the case, then biting my hand was just a way of defending herself. The perception of a person with dementia is skewed. Even if their vision is clear, HOW they perceive what they see is a different matter entirely. Because cognition is impaired, what they *think* they see (or hear) is what they will react to; not what they *actually* see or hear.

You may never have to deal with this type of situation, but if you do, please handle it delicately. Dementia sufferers can become angry, belligerent, or even violent at some point in their progression; even those whose nature under normal circumstances would be just the opposite of that. This was the case with Mrs. Rose. She was one of the most kind, thoughtful, and congenial people you'd ever want to meet; but when the ravages of the disease took hold, she must have felt like a prisoner in her own body, let alone her own home. Remember to have compassion for your loved one and don't be offended or angry with them for their behavior. Just remember that whatever you are feeling at the moment is no comparison to what they are going through. It is much worse for them, you can be sure.

At that time, I wouldn't have said that I was offended exactly, but I was definitely confused about how she could be thinking that she was being held prisoner. (I suppose it had something to do with being locked inside her house?) I say that facetiously, but in looking back now, I'd have to say, she didn't have the reasoning ability to distinguish between having the doors locked for safety reasons and being "locked in" against her will.

When a situation gets to this level of intensity, just keep it simple. Don't overwhelm them with lengthy explanations or reasoning which they no longer have the power to execute, or to understand. Speak in simple terms, like you would with children, without talking down to them.

Another example of paranoia syndrome is a story I once read about an 80 year old man named Simon. He became convinced that his daughter drove from another state and stole his dog. He tried to enlist help from his other children to get his dog back, with no success. He got so angry about it that he disinherited her. He called her constantly asking for his dog, and all the while the dog continued to live with him.

Behavioral symptoms such as these, and many others, including depression, wandering, physical aggression, or sexually inappropriate behavior, display what is referred to as, *neuropsychiatric symptoms*. They are often perplexing or troublesome to the caregiver and those close to the patient. Remembering that changes in your loved one's behavior is a result of changes in their brain, and not always their own choice, will help you to understand that the challenges presented by their behavior are not their fault and allow you to separate the person from the behavior.

Blessed are the merciful:
for they shall obtain mercy.

- Matthew 5:7

Not a Normal Part of Aging

Each caregiver wants to provide the best care possible to their loved one while preserving their quality of life for as long as possible.

Because most dementia patients eventually lose the ability to express their desires regarding care, the caregiver should encourage their loved one to communicate as much, and as early in the disease's progression as possible, about their feelings regarding their future care. Then the caregiver can be more confident in carrying out those arrangements later on.

While dementia is not yet fully understood, researchers have identified several specific onset symptoms. When a loved one begins to display behaviors that could be associated with dementia, it's time to visit a specialist. Some of these symptoms may be very subtle, others blatant. Listed below are some warning signs, in no particular order, of possible onset of dementia.

10 Warning Signs
Of Possible Dementia Onset:

1. Lapses in memory that affect normal functions
2. Problems doing normal tasks, such as cooking, bathing or dressing themselves
3. Difficulty with language; such as, "Where is...that thing I use for sweeping?" (Broom)
4. Impaired judgment
5. Lack of abstract thinking skills, like planning or understanding new information
6. Losing things

7. Disorientation and confusion with time and location
8. More frequent mood changes
9. Changes in behavior
10. A loss of initiative

It is important to note here that practically everyone has some of these issues in their everyday lives, but a person who might be suffering from dementia has more trouble with these than the average person. In dementia, the symptoms get progressively more pronounced.

Some drugs or illnesses mimic dementia symptoms and this presents a major challenge in arriving at a dementia diagnosis. Another challenge is the fact that there is so little information on how "normal" brains age.

Risk Factors

There are several diseases that warrant a dementia diagnosis. Each type of dementia has a different cause, although they all impact brain function. To treat dementia, the underlying causes must be treated. *Some of those causes are reversible*. Though the cause for each type of dementia varies, one cause that is common to many types is family history, or heredity.

10 Causes Of Dementia Symptoms Which Are Potentially Reversible:

See *Glossary* for definitions or further information

1. Normal Pressure Hydrocephalus
2. Vitamin B12 Deficiency
3. Thyroid Disorders
4. Sleep Deficits
5. Medication Side Effects or Interactions
6. Brain Tumors
7. Subdural Hematomas
8. Delirium
9. Depression (Pseudo dementia)
10. Wernicke-Korsakoff Syndrome

There are many risk factors for developing dementia symptoms. While older people are more likely to suffer dementia problems, old age, itself, does not inherently cause dementia. *Getting older is a risk factor*, but not a cause of dementia. As I said earlier, dementia is not a normal part of aging. Rather, people who develop dementia in old age usually do so because of their overall health, but especially their cardiovascular health. *People who smoke* or are physically inactive, as well as those who have *type 2 diabetes* or *high blood pressure*, are more likely to develop a form of dementia, especially Alzheimer's. Besides changing these lifestyle habits, eating well and exercising the brain - by using it - can help lower the risk of developing dementia.

People with more education are <u>less</u> likely to get, or will delay, a dementia diagnosis. People who keep their brain active are far less likely to slip into depression or social isolation and this can have a positive effect on their overall health, and particularly their cognitive health.

Socially active people are more likely to avoid or delay dementia onset. Studies have shown that engaging in social interaction on a regular basis can go a long way toward maintaining cognition. One study done by the Women's Healthy Aging Project examined the role of grandparenting in cognition and found that, among postmenopausal women, those who cared for their grandchildren one day a week scored considerably higher on cognitive tests than women who didn't.

In addition to boosting brainpower, babysitting also decreases the tendency toward depression as a result of the social interaction involved. The "more is not always better" rule applies here though, because the study also showed that those who spent five days or more minding their grandchildren scored lower on cognitive tests. (So many jokes...so little time.)

Other research from the Institute on Aging at Boston College suggests that a strong bond between grandparent and grandchild has anti-depressive benefits for both. The findings showed that the closer the relationship between grandparent and grandchild, the less likely either of them were to develop depression. The fewest symptoms of depression in seniors were found in those who both gave and received relational support.

State of residency may also play a part in risk for dementia. According to the Alzheimer's Association, people in the Midwest and northeast have a lower incidence of Alzheimer's than other parts of the U.S.

Head trauma, especially after being

unconscious, is another risk factor for dementia. It may even double a person's risk for suffering dementia. Mild discomfort type of head bumps do not count toward increased risk for dementia.

Of course, the treatment is dependent on the type and cause of the dementia. However, available treatment options only provide a slowing of the disease and not a cure.

Progressions

I wish I could give you a specific list of what to expect for your loved one at each stage of dementia, but the progression from one stage to another is often subtle and fluid. By this, I mean that the stages can fluctuate. One day your loved one may appear to be exhibiting symptoms considered to be stage 3, and the next day they may appear to be in stage 5 or stage 2. It's difficult to pinpoint exactly which symptoms and behaviors will occur in what order. Though it is human nature to want to know what to expect and try to be prepared, honestly - the closest we can come is generalities.

The stages described for Alzheimer's disease, for example, are:

Stage 1) N*o impairment*

Stage 2) V*ery mild* cognitive decline

Stage 3) M*ild* cognitive decline

Stage 4) *Moderate* cognitive decline

Stage 5) M*oderately severe* cognitive decline

Stage 6) *Severe* cognitive decline

Stage 7) *Very severe* cognitive decline

These labels, of course, can be applied to any type of dementia, as they simply describe increasing levels of severity in cognitive decline. This decline in cognitive ability, however, can present itself in many different forms in different people.

Someone (I don't remember who) once said, "If you've met one person with dementia ... you've met one person with dementia." Their point being that, though the symptoms your loved one demonstrates may be similar to the symptoms of others, they will not be exactly the same. They are unique to them as an individual. They may not display the same symptoms as someone else who is in the same stage of the same type of dementia. Each individual is unique, with different backgrounds, different life experiences, education levels, communication skills, and many other variables which, when compared side by side, simply will not be exactly the same as others. Therefore, it is an exercise in futility to try to expect the same levels of progression, or regression as other dementia patients you may be familiar with.

Whether your loved one is suffering from Alzheimer's disease or another form of dementia, the truth is, they are not going to get better. They are going to experience increasingly difficult levels of cognitive decline. This decline affects, not only their thinking and reasoning abilities, but also the different functions of their entire body. Focusing on their care and comfort then, instead of what stage they are presently in, can give them the best outcome for each day.

Evaluating the best course of care and

treatment for your loved one may include several considerations, such as the most pressing needs of the patient, as well as the caregiver and other family members. It may also be helpful to speak with the patient's medical team to explore local full-time and part-time care options. Searching for caregiver support groups, either locally or through the Internet, may be of some interest as well. Although each situation is unique and should be considered individually, there are some common threads that should be considered.

First, the person suffering with dementia has a disease and cannot help their behavior. They are not just acting out. They are often confused and frustrated, but, in the early stages especially, will usually respond well to understanding and respect.

Second, the disease will progress even with treatment. In the beginning, the patient may experience some slowing of the symptoms with available treatment options; however, currently there are not any definitive cures for dementia.

Caregivers can expect to help a patient with the activities of daily living. At first these may include things like grocery shopping and preparing meals. The patient may also need transportation and someone to attend medical appointments with them. Filling a pill reminder box and keeping track of medications may be a portion of the caregivers' tasks initially. The patient may also need help balancing their checkbook, paying their bills, and planning for their future legal and financial needs.

Symptoms will get worse and the patient will be able to do less and less of their own self-care. They may also become more frustrated and paranoid as they feel their loss of independence. In some cases, the patient may even become violent. At this point, it is best if the caregiver has already given consideration to some of the options for more direct care. *While each patient and situation is different, there are some assumptions that can help caregivers plan*. See *The Conversation.*

As the disease progresses, caregivers will need to step in more and more. As the patient gets to the place where they can no longer take care of themselves, the caregiver may have to dress, bathe and otherwise help with the patient's personal care. The caregiver will need to be aware of the patient's safety issues, such as wandering, or movement in general. The patient may need help transferring from a chair to the bed or simply walking around their home.

As the disease takes more of a toll, the caregiver will have to step in to plan for more extensive care for the patient. This may include managing other caregivers, hiring paid staff or deciding to seek residential facilities equipped to care for dementia patients. All of these decisions will be easier if the caregiver and the patient have talked about them early in the disease.

Even with dementia patients in residential facilities, caregivers remain involved, especially monitoring the needs of the patient and advocating for their care.

In some cases, symptoms may appear up to ten years before anyone notices any difficulty with cognition. Researchers are working to identify people who are in this earliest stage, as with the eye test research, where some links were found between thinning of the retinal nerve fiber layer and poor performance in cognitive tests. There is also some research being done in

London which suggests that problems identifying odors may be an indicator of future cognitive decline. If these research avenues prove to be viable, it may then be possible to slow or stop the disease more effectively by treating those early indicators. However, right now the most common symptom of dementia is loss of memory. Life expectancy from diagnosis to death is between four and eight years. This is just an average, as some patients live as long as 20 years past diagnosis.

In the early stages of dementia, whether Alzheimer's or another type, there are usually no noticeable changes in the patient's behavior or memory abilities that would alert anyone to the existence of a problem. But at this point tangles and plaques have begun to form in the brain, though not to the point of the growths doing much damage. The patient continues with their normal routine and their future caregiver is likely unaware that the disease is on the horizon. The patient's interactions are basically the same as they always have been.

As more plaques and tangles grow inside the patient's brain, they will begin to experience some memory loss. They may begin to notice a bit more forgetfulness or they seem to misplace things more often. They may notice some decline in their thinking ability, but those around them do not yet see any changes. Progressive growth of the plaques and tangles, however, will further disrupt transmission of information between brain cells. At this point, the patient may suspect that something is going on. They may find themselves trying extra hard to remember things. They may try to cover up any memory problems they are having.

Most people are diagnosed around stage four, as the disease has progressed to the point where many of those around the patient begin to notice they are having problems in social situations, memory, and language. At this point, the plaques and tangles in the brain are severely interfering with the functioning of the cortex, the area of the brain responsible for speaking and understanding. The patient gets more frustrated every time they can't think of the right word or they lose an item.

Caregivers should be supportive and ready to help when the patient asks, but not step in too much at this stage. *This is the time* the caregiver and family members should begin to discuss the patient's wishes for their later care. At this stage, the patient will still be able to understand and make informed decisions. Making these decisions, such as when to seek in-home or in-resident care, whether the patient wants feeding tubes, etc., will not only help the patient and caregivers be more comfortable as the disease progresses, it will relieve some of the questions the caregiver will have later.

As progression continues the patient will not be able to function without help. They will forget addresses and phone numbers and begin to become confused. They will remember only the people closest to them and have trouble remembering any new information. They will begin to feel more and more frustrated at having to work so hard at accomplishing normal living tasks. The caregiver will begin to see how much work and responsibility will fall to them. *This would be the time* to actively enlist help with caregiving. Explore available options and ask family members to help.

If the patient's dementia symptoms are a

result of strokes, the changes in behavior or the progression of the disease can often be more like stair steps, rather than phases. Their condition can remain unchanged for long periods until they experience another stroke. When that stroke affects additional cells, the patient may or may not experience a decline in their function.

Other types of dementia may differ in progression type or speed, but all will progress toward total incapacitation and eventual death, either from the dying of brain cells themselves, or from an infection such as pneumonia, which they have lost the ability to fight because of an otherwise weakened system.

In the latter stages the patient usually cannot function in social situations. They need help with most of the activities of daily living and will most likely experience incontinence. They may start to wander off at times, while still having periods of complete clarity. Their brain is literally shrinking, as there are fewer and fewer functioning cells, and those remaining are having a difficult time transmitting and receiving information.

The caregiver should call on those who are

willing to help. They need to make sure that they are taking care of themselves. At this point, the patient is at, or near, the point where they need 24/7 care. It is nearly impossible for one person to do everything. The caregiver should make sure they are eating well and getting enough sleep to be ready to do all the tasks necessary to help their loved one. Let me remind you, *it is not a sign of weakness to ask for help.*

In the last stage of dementia the patient loses their ability to speak. Their reflexes are not normal and they may not be able to sit, or even hold their head up. The brain mass is smaller than it has ever been. They will often curl up into a fetal position because their brain is dying but their muscles are not. This happens because the part of their brain that is still working is the part that controls the pull of the muscles, and the ones that are strongest for most people are the ones that pull them inward and forward, which pulls them into a fetal position. Most patients are not aware of the present at this point. They need full and complete care around the clock. *This is the time* when many are in resident care programs.

The dying brain also means that infections can occur because the brain is not telling the body what to do to fight it off. A fever is the signal that there is an infection in the body; but people in late stage dementia don't usually get fevers. This is because their bodies don't receive any signals from the brain to activate T-cells in order to get the white blood cell count up and give them a fever. In these cases, you would know by behavior before you would know by white cell count that there is an infection brewing. Requesting a urinary culture on your loved one to check for infection *at every doctor visit* could be your best defense against urinary tract infection, upper respiratory infection, or pneumonia.

Pneumonia is the #1 cause of death in late-stage dementia patients, closely followed by dehydration. It is important to remember that, even though dementia results from other conditions, it is still terminal. The patient may technically die from an infection or some other complication, but they were predisposed to those complications by the dementia, and rendered too weak to fight them off.

They may succumb to a blood clot in the lung from being bedridden and immobile, or an infection like aspiration pneumonia, occurring as a result of swallowing difficulties. With impaired mobility, they are at risk for several types of complications, such as the above mentioned blood clot in the lung or aspiration pneumonia.

Daily Care Situations
Practical Tips For Managing
Neuropsychiatric Symptoms

Challenging behaviors of a dementia
sufferer should always be viewed as
an attempt to communicate

Dementia patients often have a difficult time caring for themselves. As their brain cells continue to die, cognitive deficiencies will increase, which can cause them to literally forget how to do certain things they may have done thousands of times throughout their lives. Things you or I might do without even thinking about it, such as maneuvering buttons or zippers on clothing, or turning on the water in the tub or shower, might prove to be an impossible task for them. They can become agitated when they experience the frustration of not being able to do things for themselves.

You may begin to see an increase in your loved one's irritability, as well as their sleeplessness. This can also be accompanied by an increase in physical aggression and suspicion of others. As a caregiver, you can learn skills to increase your ability to help them with difficult tasks and manage difficult behaviors.

Some activities and behaviors which might present challenges are listed below with suggestions on how to make them easier to manage.

Agitation

Agitation can be triggered by a variety of things, such as fatigue, fear, or environmental factors. Usually it happens when the patient begins to feel that the caregiver is taking control away from them, which, in some ways, they are. This is why it is crucial to be delicate with them. They are already experiencing loss of abilities, so they are likely to be super sensitive to anything they perceive as an attempt to control them. During a period of agitation, *do not try to forcibly restrain them*. Instead, connect with them visually, verbally, and physically.

Visually: Approach them from their dominant side, whether right or left-handed. Most people prefer their dominant side for comfort so approaching them from this side will be less unsettling to them when trying to calm them and bring them out of an agitated state.

Verbally: Speak softly to them, acknowledging their anger and agreeing with their point of view. Use a soothing tone to help them understand that you are there to help, and to reassure them that you are on their side.

Physically: Use the hand-*under*-hand approach (*your* hand under *their* hand) to assist them in sitting, standing, or moving away from the source of agitation. This is less threatening than hand-*over*-hand, which they may interpret as an attempt to control them. See *Catastrophic Reactions*.

Tips for Reducing Agitation

- Limit the number of difficult situations your loved one must face. This can reduce the stress level for both of you.
- Support their independence and ability to care for themselves by allowing them to do as much for themselves as they can.
- Turn complex tasks into several smaller tasks by breaking them down into several simple steps. This will encourage them to do things for themselves.
- <u>Example</u>: Instead of asking them to set the table for four, ask them to set out four plates, and then ask them to set out four glasses, then four forks, etc.
- Limit sugar and caffeine. Be mindful of withdrawal symptoms, such as headaches, etc. if they have been a heavy consumer of either of these.
- Reduce clutter, noise, and the number of people in the room.

- Choose the time of day when agitation is at a minimum to complete the more difficult tasks.
- Provide a calm and comforting environment.
- Maintain structure by sticking to a predictable daily routine as much as possible. This will help reduce their feelings of being overwhelmed.
- Avoid rushed situations.
  - When you are rushing, there is anxiety, which can lead to what is referred to a "catastrophic reaction" as the person tries to figure out their next step. See *Catastrophic Reactions*.
- Cut back on television viewing. The fast-paced visual images and loud sounds can sometimes overwhelm someone with dementia.
- Remain calm and comforting; do your best to never raise your voice or argue. You set the prevailing mood of the home for your loved one.
- Never scold or make the person feel bad for their actions.
  - Trying to set them straight will only

agitate them further. At this point, the facts don't really matter. *Managing your own behavior can change the outcome of an interaction.*

- Keep rooms well-lit and at a comfortable temperature.
- Keep furniture and household objects in the same places. Familiarity offers a sense of security and can often trigger pleasant memories.
- Keep dangerous items out of reach.
- Use an activity or a snack as a distraction when you see the stress level rising.

Bathing

- Set the temperature of the water heater in your home to a temperature below 120 degrees Fahrenheit to protect from burns. Always check the temperature of the bath or shower and do not allow your loved one to change it.
- Install grab bars in the tub or shower and use a shower seat and a hand-held shower head.
- Wash their hair at a different time than when bathing or use a dry shampoo.

- Provide them as much privacy as possible by draping a towel over them when bathing, uncovering only the body part you are washing at the time. This also provides them with a sense of security in some cases.

- Always consider what your loved one's preferences are. Do they prefer a shower or a bath? Morning or evening? Two or three times a week is enough in most cases if bathing is difficult.

- Have all the bathing supplies ready at hand. Do not leave your loved one alone in the bathroom.

Eating

- Prepare meals and snacks for your loved one and gently remind them to eat. To encourage them to drink, simply hand them a cup instead of placing it on the table near them.

- If holding a glass is difficult, use a coffee mug so they can place their fingers through the handle. You can also try using a straw or even a child's sippy cup.

- Enjoy a meal with friends and family whenever you can. Eating with others around may help them to remember what to do and how to eat.

- Finger foods are a great way to encourage independence.
- Serve soup in a mug instead of a bowl.
- Instead of three large meals a day, provide smaller meals, more often.
- Offering the foods and drinks that your loved one really likes will encourage them to eat.
- Don't be concerned about them getting into a rut of eating the same thing several days in a row. If they like the food, they will eat it, and that's what is important.
- Keep plenty of nutritious foods on hand so they will have a variety and eating will be less of an issue for them.

Incontinence

- Respecting your loved one's privacy will help them to retain their dignity for as long as possible.
- Remind them or assist them, if needed, to use the bathroom every two hours.

- Watch for non-verbal cues that they need to go, such as agitation, fidgeting, or pulling on clothes.
- A raised toilet seat or grab bars are a worthy investment in your loved one's safety.
- In some cases a bedside commode could provide added convenience.
- Place signs on the walls in your home to show them the way to the bathroom.
- Use incontinence products if needed for good peri-care and hygiene.
- Wearing clothing with elastic waistbands or Velcro fasteners will make it easy for them to go quickly when needed.
- They should be encouraged to drink 6 to 8 cups of fluids each day. Limit the amount of liquid consumed in the evening between supper and bedtime and restrict caffeine or alcohol consumption.
- A diet high in fiber will help to prevent constipation.
- Keep an "overnight bag" in the car with toiletry items and a change of clothes (including undergarments) in case they don't

make it to the restroom in time when they are out in public.

Paranoia

It is unsettling to see your loved one become jealous, accusatory or suspicious. Just know that it is part of the disease and very common with dementia patients. Remember that it is very *real to them* try not to take it personally. It is best not to disagree or argue with them, no matter how bizarre their behavior may seem to you. Their reasoning abilities are diminished and trying to reason with them will only cause them more stress.

- Respond to the feeling behind the accusation, which is usually (though not always) fear. Offer reassurance by saying something like, "I can see that this bothers (frustrates, frightens, etc.) you. Stay with me, I won't let anything happen to you."
- If they suspect that money is missing, allow them to keep small amounts in a pocket or purse that they can easily locate to reassure them.

- Rather than arguing with them, offer to help them look for a misplaced object and have extra ones on hand for those things that are regularly misplaced.
- Take note of their favorite hiding places.
- Distract them with an activity to take their mind away from the agitation.
- Responding with a gentle touch or a hug will help with calming them when the agitation winds down.
- Take time to explain to caregivers, friends, and family members that this behavior is normal for the disease and there is no need for alarm.

Repetitive Speech or Action

- Ignore the behavior and distract them with an activity or a snack.
- Avoid reminding them that they just asked the same question.
- Avoid discussing future plans until just before the event.

- You can reduce agitation by putting signs on the kitchen counter or table for anticipated events, such as, "Dinner is at 6:30pm" or "Bob comes home at 5:00pm" to avoid uncertainty or anxiety about upcoming events.

Sleeplessness

- Restrict intake of sweets and caffeine later in the day.
- Plan more daytime activities. Physical exercise, such as walking, is helpful. Check with the person's doctor for appropriate activities.
- Discourage napping in the afternoon.
- Place a nightlight in the bedroom, bathroom, and hallway.
- Lock doors and block stairs with tall gates. Put away dangerous items.
- Install door sensors and motion detectors to alert you when they are wandering because of sleeplessness.
- Talk to your doctor about medicine that may help them relax and sleep. Ask if their sleeping problems are

related to dementia or another medical problem.

- Have others help with caregiving so that you can sleep. Take naps when possible to feel rested.
- Plan a structured, quiet activity in the late afternoon such as a card game or listening to music together.
- Turn on the lights well before sunset and close the curtains to reduce shadows.
- Place clocks where your loved one can see them.
- Allow them to sleep wherever they are most comfortable. Read more on this subject in the next chapter, *Sundowning*.

Sundowning

Understanding the changes in your loved one's behavior which occur with sundowning will help you anticipate how to meet their needs.

As hinted by the name, sundowning begins to take place in the late afternoon or evening and starts to occur in the mid-stages of the disease. It may manifest as confusion, increased agitation, or sometimes even hyperactivity. The personality changes may be drastic or subtle, depending on the individual. Each person is different, so how fast it comes on, how long it lasts, and how severe it is will differ. One constant is that, however the changes come, they will most likely worsen as the disease progresses.

There is no real explanation for why this happens, other than damage occurring in the brain. This is bound to cause a disruption in circadian rhythm, the internal clock of the body. This damage can interrupt the sleep-wake cycle which may cause increased irritability and confusion, resulting in changes of mood and behavior toward the latter part of the day, when fatigue begins to set in.

Think of how you might feel if you went to bed and then were awakened after only a short time, either by internal or external stimuli. You would probably become irritable, especially if you had no ability to stop it from happening over and over again. Anyone who gets thrown off their normal sleep cycle can experience fatigue and sleep deprivation, which can lead to cognitive deficits. When this happens to someone with dementia, who is operating in a diminished capacity to understand what is happening to them, they become irritable and then the cycle just repeats. This is another facet of the *time-warp syndrome* they are experiencing. They can become disoriented in regard to time, location, and surroundings, from disrupted sleep-wake cycles.

Recognizing the symptoms of sundowning is the first step in handling it with your loved one. Finding the right approach may be a trial and error process for you. Start with avoiding activities that require concentration late in the afternoon or evening, when sundowning tends to be the worst.

Doing your best to get them into a normal sleep schedule will go a long way in delaying the severity of the condition. The most effective way of doing this is to arrange their activities to keep them on a set schedule *as much as possible*. There are many benefits to this and it is well worth the effort. Routine, Routine, Routine – this is the dementia patient's best friend – for many reasons.

Did you catch that? Let me repeat - a*dhering to a routine schedule is the absolute best thing you can do for a dementia sufferer.* It provides comfort and familiarity, which is like a warm fuzzy blanket for their mind. When they are comfortable they are secure; and when they are secure, they are much calmer and more settled, as anyone would be.

Other things you can do to help reduce sundowning symptoms:

1. **Turn the lights on**. Studies show that a couple of hours each morning with a full-spectrum fluorescent light about three or four feet away from them can lighten their mood and decrease confusion and agitation.

2. **Keep them active**. Regular daytime activities, coupled with limited naps will encourage better nighttime resting and avoid fatigue, which is a common trigger for sundowning. Many of those who have trouble sleeping at night experience sundowning.

3. **Reduce their stress**. Encouraging them to enjoy calm activities in the evening can help to minimize stress levels; both for the patient and the caregiver. Reading a book may be too difficult, but listening to soothing music or snuggling with their favorite pet might be good places to start.

4. **Regulate their sleep**. As mentioned above, limiting their naps and keeping them on a routine is the best way to do this.

5. **Adjust their eating habits**. This may not be easy to do, but if you can swing it, it may help reduce sundowning symptoms. Large meals can increase their agitation or keep them up at night – especially if caffeine or alcohol is consumed late in the day. A light meal or hearty snack, rather than a heavy meal, might help them rest better at night.

Sundowning can be troubling but, as with many of the symptoms associated with dementia, planning ahead for it and being prepared is the best course of action in managing it. Keep yourself encouraged and don't give up. Keep trying different things until you find what works for you.

Word Salad

The term, *word salad*, describes the speech patterns of someone with any form of neurological disorder, whether from an injury, stroke, dementia, or other causes. As the name implies, it is disordered speech; words, phrases, or sentences that are jumbled or "tossed," like a salad. It is a mixture of confused, or seemingly random, words or phrases which the listener cannot always decipher. Sometimes the speech comes out as, "gibberish" and contains no recognizable words at all.

You may have seen examples of "word

salad" without even realizing it. Have you ever read assembly instructions for something you bought, which were translated into English from another language? You can usually recognize it because the syntax is off. Instead of saying, "Place the flat piece on top and snap it down," it may say something like, "Be plate on top and buckle." This is the type of thing they tell us to look for when trying to identify scam emails, supposedly sent to us from reputable companies. Because they are often written by non-English speaking people, and then translated by a computer, the syntax is different and fairly easy to spot.

In dementia patients, their "computer" (brain) doesn't translate the words properly because they are missing some connections, which makes it difficult to send the right messages and so their words get jumbled. In some instances, even though the words may be right, they are in the wrong order, so they come out sounding confused and often make no sense to the listener. This can be a huge problem to some, and inconsequential to others, depending on the severity of the damage to the brain.

When a dementia patient first begins to experience this problem, you may be able to figure out what they are trying to say, at least for a while. There may come a time, however, when you will no longer be able to make sense of what they say and you must look for other clues to determine what their needs are. See *Basic Caregiving*.

A variation of word salad is often used intentionally by narcissists or other manipulative people to frustrate and confuse a person with whom they are communicating. This is usually an effort to win an argument, control the outcome of the conversation, or manipulate and control the person themselves. The ultimate goal is to get the other person to question their own perceptions, and eventually, even their own judgement in general. This is commonly known as, "gas-lighting," which is a systematic psychological manipulation using broken sentences, random words, and insinuations to convince the hearer that they are mistaken, or perhaps even going crazy. See *Glossary*.

This is obviously not the case with a dementia sufferer. They are not purposely trying to manipulate their caregiver. They are trying to communicate, but the neurons in the brain are missing some connections and they simply are not able to string together the correct words to say what they want to say.

However, the impact this phenomenon can have on the caregiver can be very similar to that of a gas-lighting victim. Even though the dementia sufferer is not doing it on purpose, and has no control over when it happens, the listener can still become confused and frustrated from trying to communicate with them.

For the narcissist, word salad usually happens when they are confronted in regard to their behavior. Rather than tell the truth and abandon the lie, their brain tells them to, "fight to the death," so they begin to speak in broken sentences and exhibit a manufactured frustration that the other person doesn't believe them, often accusing them of rushing to judgement, being too suspicious, or being crazy. They use word salad as a weapon against their target to confuse and control them psychologically. This tactic often results in confusion, frustration, self-doubt, or even anger in the victim.

So . . . WHY are we talking about narcissists in a book about caregiving? Because the results are often the same.

Even though the use of "word salad" is not an intentional manipulation by the dementia patient, it can still have an impact on the caregiver which is very similar to what a narcissism victim experiences. It can catch you off guard at the wrong moment and you may react in a way that causes unneeded stress to both your loved one and yourself. It can wear you down if you are not alert to what is happening.

In a dementia patient, far from being a weapon, word salad is often "the beginning of the end," in terms of verbal communication. Unlike the manipulator, they have no control over which words they say and which ones they leave out. When the neurons in the brain begin failing to send and receive the proper messages, the dementia sufferer will begin to experience *aphasia*, deficits in speech ability. They may refer to a woman as a man, or they may see a dog and call it a cat. They are searching for the right words, but sometimes the connection just can't be made. It is not likely that those gaps will ever be bridged, but will more likely only grow larger until eventually, the patient may even lose their ability to speak altogether.

Hazel, our next door neighbor when I was growing up, was diagnosed with dementia very late in her life. She lived alone for about ten years after her husband died before suffering a stroke, causing her dementia symptoms, and going into a nursing home. She was like a grandmother to me, growing up. I used to go and see her whenever I would travel back home and, up until the last year or so of her life, she would always know who I was. She could carry on a conversation about when we were neighbors, or how her husband would always vary from his school bus route to take my sisters and me home, but she couldn't always remember what she had for lunch that day.

The last time we had a fluid conversation, was around Christmas time and she was just beginning to experience word salad, but still had her sense of humor. Her birthday was coming up on January the first, and I jokingly asked her if she was going to be a big girl now when her birthday came. Quite sheepishly, she replied, "Nooo, I'm not going to be a grown up yet. I'll only be 99!"

The last time I visited her she was bedridden and talked incessantly, but her speech was completely unintelligible. She spoke with a clear tone and in what seemed to be a fairly normal cadence, but it was all gibberish. Not one word was understandable. She would look at me and pause periodically, as if waiting for a response from me. All I could do was tell her that I was sorry I couldn't understand her. With tears running down my face, I was almost embarrassed that I couldn't do anything for her. I wished with all my heart that I could get her to laugh or tell me about her birdwatching or any number of other things we used to talk about. I felt so helpless. I can only imagine how she must have felt, trying so hard to communicate and not being able to break through. It was so strange; as if there were an invisible wall between us. I almost didn't want to leave that day because I knew I probably wouldn't get to see her again in this life. She died 8 days after her 102nd birthday. Sometimes I think of her and chuckle, thinking, well - at least she finally got to be a grown-up.

Not all dementia patients experience word salad, and those who do may vary in their patterns. Some will stick to the same words and phrases, such as asking the same questions repeatedly. Others, like Hazel, may only be able to speak gibberish. Some may not seem to have any pattern at all. There isn't really any set pattern for you to know what to expect. It is so individualized because the damage to one person's brain is not going to be the same as someone else. There are probably as many different patterns as there are dementia patients.

The best thing you can do when you begin to see your loved one struggling with word salad is to keep a good sense of humor about it. Joking, not ridiculing, but lightheartedly laughing it off, will help your loved one realize that - yes, it's a difficulty, but no, it's not the end of the world. It's natural for them to be embarrassed about it, but you can help them avoid embarrassment by learning to just chuckle about it and move on. *If they know it doesn't upset or frustrate you, and that you will be patient with them until they can get their words out, this will relieve a lot of stress all around.* Eventually, they may reach a point where they won't be able to get their words out at all, but just keep encouraging them that – hey it's ok, don't worry about it.

Something else you can do to help relieve their frustration about word salad is to play music. The part of the brain which stores and uses language is the same part that houses music. Playing familiar music for dementia patients can often stimulate the language centers in the brain and in turn, stimulate their speaking abilities.

How does it work? Many people enjoy listening to music; and they value it because of the emotions music evokes in their brain. If those emotions are positive ones, this brings a healing property into the equation that is very powerful. Have you ever had something that you saw or heard bring back a memory of something you haven't thought about in a long time? This can be especially true with music. The song you danced to at your wedding or your high school prom, might bring back pleasant memories of a certain time in your life that you perhaps haven't thought of in years. There are pathways in the brain which hold information that you may rarely access. Everything that you have ever seen, heard, or experienced in your lifetime is recorded in those pathways.

If frightened children turn up the song on the radio to drown out the sounds of their crying mother being abused in another room by their father, hearing that same song might bring back a memory and produce negative emotions in them even thirty years later. This is because the auditory stimulation and the negative emotions they felt during that traumatic experience, even if they didn't consciously connect the two, were both recorded in the pathways of their brain simultaneously, like grooves on a vinyl record.

Conversely, if there is music that a dementia patient enjoys listening to, doing so can subconsciously produce positive emotions in them. This can have an anti-inflammatory effect in their body, improving their cognition and stimulating their speaking abilities for a certain period of time. Doing this on a regular basis can yield longer lasting effects. See *Brass Tacks*.

There were many days when Mrs. Rose might be having trouble with memory or other daily tasks, but when she sat down to play the piano, those songs were just right there "on the tip of her tongue," so to speak. We would sing songs together and she could remember all the words. In the later stages this began to disappear little by little; but it was amazing to me that, even when she had difficulties with other things, she responded so well when familiar music was played or sung.

I remember hearing the story of a woman who could no longer walk or speak. She was brought in a wheel chair to the funeral of a friend and during the service a familiar hymn was sung. She began to stir and become aware and before the song ended she sang an entire verse and chorus with the congregation and then became silent again when the song ended. Even bedridden dementia patients have been known to respond to familiar music being played. I wish I had known that when I had my last visit with Hazel. I can't help but wonder if it's possible that I might have been able to bring her one more moment of clarity to say goodbye.

Catastrophic Reactions

A catastrophic reaction is an excessive response to a common, ordinary, non-threatening situation. The use of the word "catastrophic" indicates that there is a disaster, or some horrible event that occurred. "Catastrophic" is how it must feel to the person with dementia when experiencing this type of reaction to an otherwise ordinary situation.

The cause of a catastrophic reaction can be a number of things. They may simply not be feeling well or they might be feeling rushed or confused. It may be a result of an accumulation of small things throughout the day that find their way to the surface later in the day.

As the caregiver, you may naturally feel the need to defend your action or even argue, but the best thing to do in response to a catastrophic reaction is 1) *stay calm* and 2) *be reassuring*. Rather than point out the facts of the matter, simply tell your loved one that you are listening and validate their feelings. See *Daily Care Situations* for more tips on reducing agitation.

8 Steps To
De-Escalating a Catastrophic Reaction

Calming a dementia patient from an agitated state is usually a one person job. When two or more people get involved it elevates their stress level and often causes them to feel overwhelmed, which is counterproductive. Restraint and sedation are sometimes used in care facilities to bring them out of an agitated state, but trying this first can often eliminate the need for that. I'm not saying it's <u>never</u>

appropriate to sedate them, but I don't believe it should be the go-to solution. No matter how much a person with dementia "misbehaves," somewhere in there is a person wanting help. De-escalation should always be tried first.

Effective communication is essential for successful de-escalation. Body language is just as important as verbal communication, if not more so, in demonstrating your support to a dementia patient in a crisis situation. It is a <u>must</u> that the patient be able to sense your compassion.

The steps below can show you, as a caregiver, how to calm the patient and bring them out of an agitated state. Read through them several times until you can visualize the scenario and walk through the steps with confidence. They are designed to help you guide the dementia sufferer from a state of extreme agitation to a state of calm. If possible, have someone walk through them with you a few times to rehearse the body movements. Take turns being the patient and the caregiver to get a better perspective from both sides. It will be much more effective if you are comfortable with the process *before* it is ever needed. The more comfortable you are with it, the easier it will be to make it work. Remember that each step takes time, so patience is the key.

1. **Remove the threat** – The *patient often feels threatened or confused* by too many people being in the room and this increases their anxiety. Give them space by having others move far enough away to create a buffer zone.

Say something like: "OK! Wait a minute! Hold on here! Everyone just back up a little!" (This shows the patient that you are there to help them and makes it easier for them to trust you.)

2. **Identify with the patient** – *Meet them where they are* emotionally by adapting their current level of anger/frustration as your own.

Turn the same direction as they are facing, to demonstrate to them that you are, "on their side."

Agree with them, no matter how far-fetched their current reasoning is, and don't try to convince them that they are wrong.

Validate their feelings, even when the facts say otherwise. This will show them you are there to help them. You don't have to violate your conscience to agree with them. You are telling them that you understand *how they feel*, not that they are right.

Remember that *challenging behavior should always be viewed as an attempt to communicate.*

This is usually the point at which you can *determine the trigger* for the outburst by listening to what they are trying to communicate. Once you know their triggers, you can more easily avoid some of the situations that trigger an agitated state.

Say something like: "Oh! Oh! I can't believe this; doesn't it just make you so mad!? This is ridiculous! What happened here?" (This gives them the opportunity to tell you what they think the problem is.)

3. **Get at, or below, eye level** – If they are standing, *stoop a little,* if necessary, to meet their eye level. If they are sitting, *sit or kneel beside them*. Looking up at you to make eye contact can be perceived by the dementia sufferer as dominance and they will be less willing to listen to you.

Say something like: "Ok – let's just see what we can do about this. It's going to be ok; come on, come over here for a minute." (Be careful not to sound patronizing at this point.)

4. **Use "hand *under* hand"** – Place *your hand* underneath *their hand,* palm flat. Your forearm then remains under theirs to stabilize their weight when standing or walking. This offers assistance without the threat of dominance. Your hand *under* theirs offers strength and support, while your other hand can offer comfort if gently placed on top of theirs.

NOTE: Steps 5 and 6 are to be done simultaneously.

5. **Use gentle hand pumps** – Begin clasping and unclasping their hand with your bottom hand, mimicking their heartbeat. Start at a faster pace which matches their current heart rate, and *gradually slow the pace* until you reach a more reduced heart rate.

6. **Breathe in sync** – The goal here is to *get the patient to breathe in sync with you* so you can guide them in slowing their breathing and heart rate. Begin by taking a big (and obvious) breath in through the nose and blowing it out through

the mouth forcefully. After you have done this 2 or 3 times the patient will subconsciously begin to do it with you. If they don't, you might gently coax them by saying something like, "Come on; breathe with me. It's going to be ok. You're ok." Watch their breathing and then gradually slow the pace of breath and hand pumps simultaneously.

7. **Relax body/Calm voice** – Use soothing tones to give assurance. "Good... there you go, you're ok. I'll take it from here." You are assuring them that you are taking care of the problem and they don't need to worry about it any longer.

8. **Attend to needs** – At this point you will be able to gently direct the patient to comply. After this kind of expenditure of energy, they may need to lie down or take a short rest. Be careful not to let them sleep too long during the day. For more on napping, see the section on *Sundowning.*

Caring For The Caregiver

Caregivers face challenges from every direction, including from within. They have the normal stresses of everyday life, just like anyone else; but with the added stress of having someone else who is fully dependent upon them.

One of the greatest strengths caregivers have can also be their greatest weakness if not properly guarded. That is, that they are generally giving and self-sacrificing people. So much so at times, that they forget to take care of themselves, and while they are probably painfully aware of this - the non-caregivers in their life may not be. They must learn not to hold it against others who may be unaware of the added stress on them, as caregivers.

So, caregivers - take care of your loved one, knowing they cannot reciprocate, and then find your respite when needed, on your own. You will find this to be much more satisfying than dwelling on the disappointment of unmet expectations of others. If you find yourself thinking, "Oh! I just wish..." it may be time to arrange a replacement for the day and go get a massage or at least a very long lunch.

A person suffering with dementia needs round-the-clock care. It is sometimes difficult and demanding for one, or even several people, to provide this level of care day after day for weeks, months, and years. Last year nearly two thirds of dementia patient caregivers reported high or very high stress. One third reported depression symptoms. About half reported family and financial strain and 75% said that there was no right or wrong answer as to the question of when, or whether, to put the patient in a nursing, or other residential care facility. Notably, 72% said they felt relief when the person passed away.

If this is you, you needn't feel guilty about it. It is a natural response to feel relief when responsibilities that have weighed heavily on you are discontinued. It does not mean that you loved that person any less. It only means that you are human. It is very difficult to watch someone you love regress to the point of helplessness, and it is a relief to know that they are no longer suffering. Once some time passes, and you are able to separate your love for that person from the feelings of stress you felt taking care of them, you will also be able to put the rest of it into perspective as well. You need not carry an unnecessary burden of guilt over being relieved of your caregiving duties.

Caregivers often neglect themselves and don't take the time they need for themselves in order to rest and re-invigorate. They skip meals and put their own needs aside, often ending up overwhelmed and frustrated. Sometimes, the caregiver feels like they are neglecting other loved ones and obligations in order to fulfill the caregiving responsibilities they have taken on, further leading to that sense of helplessness, stress, or ineffectiveness.

When a caregiver reaches the point of feeling like he or she is inadequate, they may feel as if they are betraying the loved one with dementia. The caregiver begins to see all the things that are not going quite right and they forget about all the things that are going well. This is the time when caregivers need to recognize that they need to seek help and look for resources to step in and offer a respite, even if it's just for a few hours.

Alarm at the dementia patient's actions or disease progression can affect the caregiver as well. While caregivers try to be as flexible as possible, the very nature of dementia causes strange and unpredictable behavior. Even the most adaptable caregiver is astonished sometimes. For instance, Simon, the man who was convinced that his daughter took his dog, asked his caregiver/wife to shoot him and then kill herself. He even loaded the gun and insisted that she take it from him. She did take it, for his own safety, and realized at that point that she was in over her head, and sought out professionals to help her with his care.

Then there are the legal and financial issues caregivers must face. Things like living wills, residential care, estate planning, and whether or not to let the patient continue driving; these are all common concerns.

Financial issues may begin with the patient not remembering how to count out the correct money for a purchase, or may be as complicated as not paying their utilities for months. That's when the caregiver must become the patient's banker and financial advisor in addition to all the other tasks. There are many aging care organizations that are there to help. *Don't wait.* Contact someone who can help if you need this kind of assistance.

As for legal arrangements, most require a person to be able to understand the information. Therefore, it is best to take care of any document changes as soon after the dementia diagnosis as possible. As the disease progresses it may be too demanding for the patient to comprehend enough of the explanations to make informed decisions about his or her own care or the disposition of assets.

In addition to believing that his daughter stole his dog, Simon was also convinced that the bank was stealing his money. One of his daughters investigated the situation and found that Dad was wrapping cash in foil and throwing it in the wastebasket.

These are just a few of the types of challenges caregivers can face. So listen to me, caregiver - you absolutely MUST learn to take care of yourself – so that you can be healthy and more able to take care of your loved one. If you have chosen to care for them, then give them your best. The flight attendant on an airplane tells you that in case of an emergency, you need to put your mask on first so you can then help others. In this same way, you must take care of yourself first, so that you can adequately care for your loved one. See *Caregiver's Self-Assessment Chart.*

Brass Tacks
Straight Talk to the Caregiver

In the last chapter we talked about you, as the caregiver, taking care of yourself in order to be the best caregiver you can be. Now let's talk about some stressful situations that might arise and pin down some ways to manage them.

The word "tack" is an interesting and versatile word. It is both a noun and a verb, and has several different definitions and usages. The one which applies here is: *a way of dealing with something; an approach to accomplishing a goal; a method of dealing with a problem.* Its closest synonym would be "tactic." The tacks listed below are also versatile. They are effective solutions when used for the problem situations they are listed under, but of course, they are versatile enough to be used in *many* other situations as well.

The expression *brass tacks* is used as a metaphor for "getting down to basics," or "getting down to business." It was brass tacks which were pushed into the counter of a draper's shop to provide more precise measurement than the previous method of holding one end to the nose and stretching out the arm for an approximate measure of a yard.

So let's get down to "brass tacks" then, and talk for a minute about something which influences everything you do as a caregiver. This one thing is the basis of how you will handle every situation that arises. Based on this, I have listed below a few things you may experience as a caregiver, and I've given you some tacks for dealing with them well.

Emotions

Family caregivers often perform many of the tasks and duties of fully trained nurses. One challenge they have, however, which professional caregivers usually don't, is dealing with their own emotions. Being more emotionally invested in their loved one's care, the family caregiver can sometimes become irritable, angry, or frustrated from dealing with their incapacitated loved one. Then they often heap guilt on top of that for feeling that way, and suddenly you've got a recipe for a volatile situation.

Negative Emotions

The last thing a caregiver needs is to be overtaken with an emotional response to something their loved one says or does. This is not helpful for either of you. So consider the possibilities in advance and equip yourself with these tacks so they don't sneak up on you or catch you off guard.

Emotion #1 - Frustration:

You don't need to pretend to be a saint. No one expects you to be perfect. You have volunteered to give your time and attention to someone you care about. You ARE a good person - so DO NOT feel guilty for getting frustrated with your loved one for forgetting to do things, or refusing food or meds, or soiling the bed sheets, or any number of other things that could happen. You're human; it's natural to become frustrated sometimes. It's OK to BE frustrated. It's NOT OK to take it out on others. But now that you know it's going to happen, you can meet it at the door and usher it out before it takes hold.

Tack #1 – Gentleness:

If you find yourself getting frustrated with your loved one - just take a minute - and say to yourself, "is this REALLY that big a deal?" Sometimes – yes, it IS a big deal - for safety or other reasons. Sometimes, though, thinking about how you would handle a similar situation with a small child can help. Then adapt that response to the present situation with your loved one. *Am I saying you should treat your loved one like a child?* NO! I'm saying you should treat them with the tenderness you would give to a child - whom you realize may not know any better - while still allowing them to retain their dignity as an adult.

For those times when they are stubborn, as a willful child might be, and you have to be stern with them, insisting they comply for their own good; *this is when gentleness will be its most effective.* A parent might acknowledge the wishes of the child, while still exhibiting strength to make sure the child knows that, "No. I realize *that* is what you want, but _this_ is what we're doing." That can all be accomplished, often without even saying it, simply by exhibiting resolve, but with gentleness. Knowing in your own heart that your knowledge of what the patient needs goes beyond their own understanding of it will allow you to leave behind the frustration and guide them. The grace of gentleness will overshadow any asperity of sternness, for the both of you.

Emotion #2 - Fear/Worry:

Don't be apprehensive about things going wrong, or what someone's reaction might be to how you handled a situation. Worrying about things that haven't even happened yet zaps your energy for dealing with the things that actually ARE happening. If you are a worrier, learn to let that go, at least until there is a more convenient time to do your worrying. Saying to yourself, "I'll worry about that later," may help you in learning to defer your worry. You may find that you actually do worry about it later; or you may forget about it completely.

Tack #2 – Reality Check:

If something does go wrong, be careful not to be defensive in order to protect yourself from emotional pain. Everyone makes mistakes, and it's ok to say, "I could have handled that differently" and then try another approach next time. Believe me when I say, there will usually be a next time.

Emotion #3 - Anger:

You may be taking care of someone you have known all your life; perhaps a parent, grandparent, aunt or uncle. No one is saying it's always easy to get along with a family member. There are emotional entanglements with them that professional caregivers do not have to deal with. However, if you have taken on the role of caregiver for them, most likely there is enough of a bond there to sustain you through a tough situation.

Tack #3 – Calmness:

Steer the conversation toward a more calm direction. Remember to be cheerful whenever you can without forcing it. When caregivers are tired, anxious, or already angry about something else going on in their lives, they are much more susceptible to stress. Try to replace those negative feelings with appreciation and thankfulness. It might be helpful to remember an earlier time in your loved one's life when perhaps they did something especially kind or helpful to you. Take a moment to be thankful for that, and you may find yourself with a treasure trove of memories that you can share with your loved one the next time they need some calming conversation. This will do more for dissolving anger and fostering a better relationship between you and your loved one than you might imagine. A calm assurance that *all is well* is probably the best tool you have in your emotional toolbox.

Emotion #4 - Resentment:

It's hard when they tell you they can manage something, like buttoning their clothes, for instance, or making the bed - and then suddenly they can't. They might even snap at you for trying to help them - and then turn around and snap at you for NOT helping them. THAT can be frustrating! Left unchecked, it can cause resentment to build, which could eventually turn into anger or bitterness.

Tack #4 – Sympathy:

Remember that your loved one is only responding to their perception of how things are in their world at any given moment, as we all do. Try to share in their present feeling and understand that anyone might have the response they did if they perceived it the same way as your loved one did. The problem here for dementia sufferers is that their perception is skewed. Therefore, their reactions may be inappropriate for the present situation.

Emotion #5 - Sadness:

You may become sad when you think of losing your loved one to the disease with which they are afflicted. You may even begin to feel like there is something wrong with you for feeling that way. This is normal. Experiencing sadness while caring for someone who is dying is absolutely normal.

Tack #5 – Comfort:

Focusing on caring for them today and not worrying about tomorrow or what will happen in the future can sometimes get you through the day, but it is not always a bad thing to make room for your sadness either. Read the chapter on *Grief* for more information about this.

Having a Plan

A good way to handle many of these negative emotions is to make sure there is always a tack in place. Emotional responses are a natural part of our makeup as human beings. This is the way we were designed by our Creator to deal with the everyday occurrences in life, both good and bad. *Having a plan* to help you manage your stress just makes good sense.

Having a Plan "B"

Having a "Plan B" is often a good idea too, for those rare times when the stress has gone unchecked for too long. Sometimes, just knowing that there <u>is</u> a "Plan B" is enough to keep you encouraged.

"Plan B" Tacks to Consider:

If you are the sole caregiver*:* Check with your local elder care centers to ask about meeting with a few different *respite caregivers* to find one or two you feel comfortable with, who can be *on call* to fill in for you, should the need arise.

__If you are part of a caregiving team__: Assign one of the team members as the designated relief person in case an emergency arises. The details of your alternate plan will vary, depending on the actual situation. Have some discussions with your caregiving team coordinator about what possibilities might exist for providing backup for your caregivers.

__Backup__: Always have a backup person "on call" in case a situation arises where the caregiver needs assistance or relief.

__Short Shifts__: It is much easier for three people to cover one 4 hour shift each than for one person to cover a 12 hour shift.

__Pre-Planning__: Bring a meal that you cooked ahead of time instead of trying to prepare a meal while attending to the patient at the same time.

Positive Emotions

We've discussed several negative emotions in this chapter to be aware of and guard against. However, let's not leave out the other side of the coin. Let's talk about some of the positive emotions involved in taking care of a loved one.

A few years ago I was doing some research for a behavioral science class which led me to a discovery about the connection between positive emotions and something called, "cytokines." Cytokines are proteins secreted by cells which facilitate communications between other cells and signal the immune system to work harder. There are both *pro*-inflammatory and *anti*-inflammatory cytokines. Both kinds are crucial to our health because they help us fight off infections and viruses and help wounds to heal when injury or trauma occurs. An over-production of them, however, leads to chronic inflammation, which contributes to a variety of negative health conditions, such as arthritis, type 2 diabetes, heart disease, depression, and even Alzheimer's disease and other forms of dementia. We want these cytokines in our system - just not too many.

There is a growing amount of research showing that good health comes, not only from our diet and exercise habits, but also from our emotional state of mind. Our emotions and emotional health can play a big part in our overall physical stamina.

One of the research projects I reviewed asked 200 young adults to take notes on the positive emotions they experienced throughout their day, such as amusement, contentment, awe, compassion, pride, joy, and love. Then they took cheek swabs of all the participants at the end of the day and compared the positive emotion ratings with their levels of cytokines.

What they found was amazing. The people with the highest levels of positive emotions had the lowest levels of pro-inflammatory cytokines. I found it fascinating also, that the most powerful positive emotion, yielding the lowest levels of pro-inflammatory cytokines, was found to be *awe*. Awe is the feeling of being in the presence of something bigger than we are; something vast, which goes beyond our understanding.

Seeking awe, wonder, and beauty creates healthier levels of cytokines in our system. This means that the things we do to experience these positive emotions have a definite and direct influence on our health and life expectancy. We can actually choose to do certain activities that will literally make us feel better physically.

Before reviewing this research, I had no

idea that negative emotions, even when derived from pain itself, could actually <u>cause</u> inflammation to occur in the body. I can see how that could become a vicious cycle. Inflammation, I was told, was a major hindrance to my healing from a surgery I had a few months prior. After learning about the connection between positive emotions and cytokines, I began to apply the principle to my own life and it proved to be extremely beneficial in several different ways, not the least of which was overall better health.

Putting this information in the context of dementia caregiving, I believe that if the caregiver can find ways to help the patient experience positive emotions *every day*, it will go a long way toward promoting better overall health for them, as well as a better state of mind. Doing activities two or more times a week which evoke positive emotions from your loved one can yield results that will last for several weeks. Doing it on a continual basis then, will continue to make deposits into their cognitive bank and keep them more alert and active for longer.

Take your loved one for a short walk, or sit with them on the porch and watch the birds and squirrels. Enjoy some art together or listen to some music they like. In addition to those positive emotions named in the study, try to experience as many as possible of these with your loved one each day:

- Happiness
- Joy
- Calmness
- Appreciation
- Gratefulness
- Cheerfulness
- Enthusiasm
- Hope

The anti-inflammatory effect it will have on their body will benefit them greatly.

This, of course, applies to you as well. Find something that awes you, or makes you experience wonder, and spend some time with it every day. For some, it is their relationship with God; for others it may be enjoying nature, looking at art, or listening to music. Whatever it is in your life that puts you in a state of awe, try to experience it every single day. It will make you a happier, healthier, and more pleasant person - and a better caregiver as well.

As caregivers, we want as much time with our loved one as possible. Review the tacks given above and experiment with activities and conversations that evoke positive emotions in your loved one. I think you will be pleased with the results.

"A merry heart doeth good like a medicine: but a broken spirit drieth the bones."

\- Proverbs 17:22

The Conversation

Courage is the power to let go of the familiar.
                                        - Raymond Lindquist

Remember, the person suffering with dementia is not a child who is acting up to get attention; they have a disease and it is not within their power to control their own behavior. They are having trouble coping with everyday life, and yet, at times they are painfully aware that their involvement in once enjoyable activities is diminishing. This causes further confusion and anxiety. These feelings often cause great distress for the patient, as well as the people close to them.

As previously discussed, the first consideration for a caregiver in regard to future care, is to begin talking with the patient about it when they are first diagnosed. At this point, no matter what the diagnosis, the patient probably has times of complete clarity and understanding. Their desires for their own care are the priority of this discussion. The patient and the caregiver should explore together who will be offering care and what other community support options are available.

The bonds created and/or strengthened by this conversation will be of great benefit to both the patient and the caregiver. The patient will empirically know that they have a partner and dedicated advocate to see them through the future. The caregiver will know what the desires of the patient are, and will be better able to form a plan that includes the patient's wishes for future care and treatment. For both of them, this conversation is relieving.

Ironically, both the patient and the caregiver may be reluctant to begin this conversation. They are each experiencing their own form of denial, or coping with the diagnosis. The caregiver can take the initiative with support from the medical or a spiritual team.

A good place to begin is eye-to-eye and at the same physical level, the caregiver and the patient discussing equally, and with respect, the patient's wishes. The caregiver should allow the patient to direct the conversation as much as possible. The patient is probably used to being in control and in charge of their own life and maybe in charge, at some point, of the now-caregiver's life.

Consider, for instance, the patient as an aging parent and one or more caregivers as that patient's children. That parent cared for and nourished their children for years. Now the children are stepping up to care for the parent and the caregivers must now evaluate themselves in their new role.

That is only one possible scenario. Whatever

type of relationship exists between you, the caregiver, and the patient, this conversation, though it may be difficult to begin, is an important one. No matter the difficulty, just know that once it has taken place, both of you will have the peace of knowing what needs to be done in the future.

This provides the caregiver with the confidence to know that they are carrying out the patient's wishes; and it gives the patient peace in knowing that the caregiver understands their desires for future care and final arrangements.

Grief

**To every thing there is a season, and a time to
every purpose under the heaven: A time to
weep, and a time to laugh; a time to mourn,
and a time to dance.**

- Ecclesiastes 3:1, 4

Another aspect that bears discussion is the
reaction of the caregiver and the patient to the
dementia diagnosis. They often experience

something known as preparatory grief, or anticipatory grief.

Though not discussed nearly as often as regular grief, preparatory grief is a normal process and one that should be considered, especially when the patient and the caregiver/loved one are both fully aware of the prognosis. It is just as real, and just as intense as grief that is felt after the death of a loved one, but some people grieve before the death, experiencing the loss as it happens.

Normal grief comes after the actual loss. A person may feel depression, shock or anger at the loss they have experienced. These are all normal feelings which dissipate with time. Preparatory grief is different, in that it comes from the person imagining their life without their loved one and missing them before they are even gone. Fear often accompanies this anticipated loss, especially in women; fear of being alone or losing independence or social standing. Even the dying person may experience this preparatory grief, in the form of isolation or a sense of fear.

Whatever form it takes - *grief is a gift*. It is a

natural and healthy response to a loss. When it comes before the loss actually takes place, it is a way to make it through the transition from one way of life to another. Preparatory grief allows us to celebrate our loved one while they are still with us and can be cathartic, or cleansing, allowing us to remember all the good things about our loved one and then let them go and look toward the future. No matter how difficult that may seem at the moment, life does go on after the loss of a loved one.

You may be experiencing preparatory grief if you are experiencing any of the following: loneliness, anger, or anxiety; or perhaps guilt, fear, or emotional numbness. Fatigue, sadness, forgetfulness, or poor concentration may also be present, in addition to sadness, tearfulness, or depression. It is important to note that the patient who recognizes that they are dying will often experience similar symptoms.

So, if you are experiencing what you suspect may be signs of preparatory grief, take courage in the fact that this type of grief is normal and it will not last forever. If you believe in God, then you may have hope of seeing your loved one again someday. Either way, acknowledge your feelings of pain and loss, and realize that they are normal for your situation. Most importantly, don't be afraid to let yourself feel the pain or grief. If you are having trouble coping with your feelings, reach out to someone you trust and share your feelings with them. Take care of yourself, both physically and emotionally, and make the most of the time you have left with your loved one. Stay connected to the person you are losing, while you are in the process of losing them. The gift of preparatory grief is that you have the opportunity to make the remaining time meaningful for yourself and for them.

For caregivers experiencing preparatory grief, remember to take some time for yourself. Eat nutritious foods, exercise, drink clear fluids and get plenty of rest. These may sound impossible at some stages of caregiving, especially as fatigue, insomnia, lack of appetite, and worry begin to set in. This may be the time for the caregiver to recruit a caregiver of their own. Perhaps a spouse, friend, masseuse, or personal trainer; a counselor, pastor, or other spiritual advisor might meet this need. As with the patient, a caregiver must take care of the symptoms first.

With the caregiver more able to cope with all of the pressures involved, they can now focus on caring for their loved one.

"No passion so effectually robs the mind of all its powers of acting and reasoning, as fear."
- Edmund Burke

Wandering

Wandering is an interesting concept, isn't it? It is usually considered to be passive in nature, often with no clear purpose; or at least no KNOWN purpose to the casual observer. The common phrase, "wandering around aimlessly" expresses what most people think of when they hear the word "wandering." We are fascinated by the "Wayfaring Stranger" in the famous song of the same name, the "Stranger" and the

"Wanderer" of the old western movies, and the "Pilgrims," of our early American heritage.

The carefree or adventurous nature of the human spirit, common to all of us in one way or another, is often the image conjured up when we think about wanderers. Wanderers are looking for something. Sounds simple, doesn't it? Wandering is a curious behavior; or perhaps I should say, a behavior of the curious.

Behavior is a clue to what people are feeling. When they laugh, cry, or show some other emotion, it's usually an indication of what is going on inside. When they wander, it's an indication that they are searching for something. Wandering is present in many areas of life. We read about wanderers in the Bible, and wandering has been the subject of literature for many years.

The writer's mind "wanders" into strange and unfamiliar territory to discover what happens next in their yet unwritten story. A spouse may "wander" from their marriage, searching for something they feel they don't have in their relationship. Moral judgments aside here, the fact is that they are searching for something; something which, in their mind, holds some level of significance.

When a dementia sufferer wanders, they are also seeking something. It may or may not be tangible. They may be looking for a person, a place, or even a different time frame from their own life. They may be saying they "want to go home," when they are sitting in their own living room. Because their memory is failing them, they can't always explain to us what it is they actually feel they need. They just have an inner desire to "go find it." Exactly what IT is, they don't always know, but when dementia-driven wandering begins to happen, it is an indication that they are experiencing an inner agitation of some sort. They may be experiencing dissatisfaction with someONE or someTHING in their life - so they start looking for a way out. It could also be simple curiosity or boredom that leads them to start wandering. As a result of the memory loss, however, they may have difficulty knowing where they want to go, or even WHY they want to go, or how to get back.

It may seem random to the onlooker, but there is usually a reason hidden in there somewhere. Unlocking the mystery or origin is another story altogether.

Wandering, or "roaming", as some call it, can quickly become a safety issue and should never be taken lightly. *At the first sign* of wandering, take precautions in the home to prepare for what may be coming up next.

"What 'fires' will I be putting out today?" one caregiver asked. Though she didn't mean a literal fire, of course, sometimes you do have to look at it this way in order to keep yourself alert and on top of things. Being prepared is extremely important. Many potential hazards, including an *actual* fire, can be avoided with just a little forethought and precaution. Just be careful, however, that you do not LIVE on full alert all the time without some occasional relief and respite. See *Caring for the Caregiver.*

Signs that your loved one may be at risk for wandering:
- Increased Restlessness
- Pacing
- Agitation
- Inability to stay on task

- Forgetting where they are
- Needing to be reminded where the bedroom or bathroom is
- Not recognizing their house anymore
- Not remembering to come back inside when they are outside
- Saying things like:
  - I have to go to work
  - I want to go home
  - I need to go shopping

There are many things you can do to prevent or delay wandering. Some of them take a lot of time and/or effort – but not nearly as much as searching for them once they've wandered off, not to mention the risk to their health and safety.

You can begin by trying a few things from this list to help your loved one who may be showing signs of an emerging tendency to wander.

Things you can do to help prevent or delay wandering:
- Do some type of physical activity each day.

- Identify the time of day when wandering usually occurs. Plan an activity during that time.
- Have continual supervision for your loved one.
- Avoid busy places, like large stores and shopping malls, which might lead to confusion.
- Provide a safe place for them to wander in, such as an enclosed back yard.
- Place a barrier in front of the door, such as a drape to hide it, or a stop sign, a "DO NOT ENTER" sign, or a piece of furniture.
- Disguise the doorknob by covering it with a strip of cloth or add child-safe plastic covers.
- Keep car keys out of sight.
- To alert you when your loved one leaves a certain area, install an alarm system or tie some empty cans to the doorknob.
- In some cases, a black mat placed in front of your door going to the outside may look like a hole to them, discouraging them from trying to go out the door.

- Items such as the person's coat, wallet/purse or glasses should be put well out of sight. They may not want to leave without those items.

Possible causes for wandering:
- Medication side effects
- Anxiety
- Boredom or listlessness
- Overstimulation

Planning Ahead:
Prep Tips for When Wandering Begins

If your loved one does wander, and you need to call the police to help locate them, the following will be helpful:

Use the *Emergency Medical Information Form* in the back of this book to record all of your loved one's current medical information, and update it regularly. Take a photo of it with your cell phone so you'll always have the information with you. Then place the paper copy, along with a current photo of your loved one, inside a clear plastic sleeve or baggie and keep it in an easily accessible place. Taping it to the refrigerator door or the inside of the front door (or both) might be good places. This can also serve as convenient places for the information to be available to caregivers in case of an emergency. Keep copies in the glove box of your vehicle also.

- Sew ID labels into their clothing and/or have them wear an ID bracelet.

- Consider registering them with the Comfort Zone, Safe Return, Project Lifesaver, or other wandering programs.

- Consider purchasing a device that uses GPS (global positioning systems) to make it easier to locate them if they wander or get lost.

- Let the neighbors know about your loved one's wandering behavior and give them your phone number.

- Make your doctor aware of the wandering. There may be a medical problem that is causing the troubling behavior.

- Remember that *behavior is a clue to what your loved one is feeling*. Be creative and flexible as you respond to their needs.

End-Stage Care

The biggest obstacle to effective care for end-stage dementia patients is their decreasing ability to effectively express their symptoms. Their ability to communicate is often so diminished that symptoms can go under-recognized, and thereby, under-treated.

End-stage patients often display troublesome or puzzling behavior. If they are in pain, but unable to tell you verbally, they may be trying to tell you through their actions. Their behavior might be their only way of communicating their pain to you. It is important to realize that *physical pain may be the root cause* of behavioral symptoms. Assessing the behavioral symptoms in dementia patients is critically important to proper pain management. See *Basic Caregiving.*

Simply treating the behavioral symptoms of a patient - responding to the behavior without questioning the reason for it - is a tragic error. That's like punishing a child for something they did without first trying to determine their reasoning. When difficult behavioral symptoms are present, search for the cause of the behavior before treating it. If the cause is pain, managing the pain properly may render behavioral management a moot point.

Continual assessment of behaviors helps pinpoint physical issues that would otherwise go unattended. Notice here, the difference between *behavior assessment* and *behavior management.*

Caregivers can learn how to observe and assess the pain levels of their loved one using the assessment scale below. Once you are familiar with it, you will begin to automatically notice the assessment components and be better able to make decisions regarding the immediate needs of your loved one.

Assessment Instructions: Observe the patient for 5 minutes before scoring his or her behaviors. The patient can be observed under different conditions (e.g., at rest, during a pleasant activity, during caregiving, and after the administration of pain medication). Score the behaviors according to the chart below. Definitions are provided in the glossary.

Scoring: The total score ranges from 0 to 10 points.

A possible interpretation of the scores is:
- 1 to 3 = Mild pain
- 4 to 6 = Moderate pain
- 7 to 10 = Severe pain

Possible causes of pain behind behavioral changes
- Infection
- Constipation
- Pressure ulcers (bed sores)
- Procedures performed

Behaviors which indicate possible pain in dementia patients

- Changes in appetite
- Irritability
- Restlessness
- Agitation
- Combativeness
- Confusion

Behaviors which indicate necessity for medical assessment

- Moaning
- Crying
- Grimacing
- Guarding

PAIN ASSESSMENT SCALE For Patients In Advanced Dementia				
Behavior	0	1	2	Score
Breathing independent of vocalization	Normal	• Occasional labored breathing • Short period of hyperventilation	• Noisy labored breathing • Long period of hyperventilation • Cheyne-Stokes respirations	
Negative vocalization	None	• Occasional moan or groan • Low-level speech with a negative or disapproving quality	• Repeated troubled calling out • Loud moaning or groaning • Crying	
Facial expression	Smiling or inexpressive	• Sad • Frightened • Frown	• Facial grimacing	
Body language	Relaxed	• Tense • Distressed pacing • Fidgeting	• Rigid • Fists clenched • Knees pulled up • Pulling or pushing away • Striking out	
Consolability	No need to console	• Distracted or reassured by voice or touch	• Unable to console, distract, or reassure	
			Total Score	
Copyright © 2013 AMDA, all rights reserved – Used by Permission				

124

Dementia patients who are having pain will sometimes exhibit agitation. In many cases, it is their way of communicating to others that they are experiencing pain. Sadly, in care facilities, they are frequently treated with psychotropic medications or restraints instead of having a thorough behavioral and pain assessment done. It may be up to you, the caregiver, in such cases, to advocate for your loved one and insist that an assessment be done before treatment is administered for behavioral symptoms.

Whether your loved one is being cared for in the home or in a care facility, there are a few things to consider that will relieve their pain and stress, and thereby many of the undesirable behavioral symptoms. Among them are:

8 Ways To Reduce Pain And Stress
- Massage therapy
  - neck rubs, foot rubs, or full body massages
- Reflexology
  - manipulation of pressure points on hands and feet
- Music therapy
- Art therapy
- Reading to them

- Deep breathing exercises
- Relaxation techniques
- Spiritual guidance

As mentioned before, it's a good idea to have advance care directives in place so that the hospice care and/or palliative care providers can carry out the wishes of the patient. The best time to do this is as soon after diagnosis as possible. See *The Conversation*.

Understanding the difference between palliative care and hospice care can be a challenge. They are very similar and often overlap. The central issues in both are comfort, pain management, and quality of life. So - what is the difference? In theory, the lines are clear; but in practice it's a bit more ambiguous. Some considerations are the aggressiveness of the disease, available care and treatments, and even insurance or care facility regulations in some cases.

Whatever the care situation, here's a good little mnemonic device to help you remember the difference between the two types of terminal care.

*P*alliative *"Pushes back"* the disease, while *Hospice "Hosts it."*

Palliative care offers comfort and relief of symptoms while still aggressively treating the disease, "pushing back" the effects of the disease with medications or other treatments unless, and until, it is determined that the possibility no longer exists for cure.

Hospice care is similar to palliative care, but with one main difference. The goal is no longer recovery or cure for the patient, but one of comfort and relief of pain. Hospice care then, "hosts" the patient, meeting their needs and making them as comfortable as possible, as with palliative care, with medications or treatments, but no longer pushing the symptoms back or delaying progression.

Hospice care is appropriate when the medical professionals who are treating the patient are in agreement that life expectancy is six months or less. When to begin hospice care is ultimately the patient and their family's decision, but the recommendation by the medical staff is usually a prerequisite to considering it.

When my brother reached the point of needing hospice care, he opted for in-home hospice because he didn't want to spend his last days in a hospital bed. He tried his best to keep up his regular daily activities of life, but one by one he had to stop doing some things because he simply had no energy to do them any longer. He would spend 3 or 4 hours a day planning and strategizing all that he was going to do that day in his garden, pulling weeds, picking tomatoes, green onions, peppers, and other things. He knew that once he got outside he would only have about 10 to 15 minutes before he would be worn out so he meticulously planned each step. He said it was easier, and much more enjoyable, doing the planning than the actual execution of the tasks. His wife could have easily done that for him but it was his only physical activity for the day so he tried to do it himself for as long as he could. He had a rare form of bone cancer called myelofibrosis and the pain was often overwhelming.

One day he told me, "Hospice comes and checks my vitals and tries to palm off oxygen and drugs 'cause there's nothing else they can do I guess. I just tell them, 'I don't need anything, I'm about the same as last time' . . ." My sister called two days later to tell me he had died.

Each individual must decide for themselves what works for them, in terms of the kind of end-stage care they want to have. Some want to die in a hospital with doctors and nurses around them with round the clock care up to their last breath. Others, like my brother, want to be at home and simply *go gentle into that good night.* (Dylan Thomas). Neither is the wrong choice. Everyone comes to their own conclusion on the matter.

We've talked about taking care of the caregiver, making sure you are in good health, and staying strong enough to care for your loved one. I would be remiss, though, if I didn't tell you also, to consider your spiritual health even more than the physical. Please make sure you have made preparation for your soul before you go. *How you die* is not nearly as important as *where you go* once you've gone.

The advantage (if there is one) of having a terminal illness is having, "advance notice" that you are dying so that you CAN make sure you know where you will go – and you CAN know.

1John 5:13 says, "*These things have I written unto you that believe on the name of the Son of God; that ye may <u>know</u> that ye have eternal life, and that ye may believe on the name of the Son of God.*"

Not that we don't all know we will die someday, but the opportunity to contemplate life, death, and *life after death* is a gift, not to be overlooked.

If both you and your loved one have a personal relationship with God, you will be together again after this time of dementia has passed. Neither one of you will be stressed or tired or forgetful or weary, and you can recount the days you spent together when they were sick and you cared for them.

If you don't have a personal relationship with God, you CAN if you want to. You only need to ask. He is so very willing to make it so, and will answer when you call.

Feel free to contact me personally if you would like someone to walk you through it. I would count it my honor to do so.

THE RANSOM

Came Death's Angel to my door,
'Twas ill forebodings that he bore,
"What is wrong?" to him I said,
He answered, "Here, 'tis thy death-bed"

As he left my thoughts returned
To the life for which I yearned;
'Twas not for life with natural breath,
But for the life that's after death.

I knew that peace which God had promised
To the ones who do His work;
Those who great things do accomplish,
Do not fear, and do not shirk;

So I sought His boundless grace,
Notwithstanding, I was weak;
And before me came His face,
Saying, "Learn of me, for I am meek"

Then Salvation, God's great gift,
To my heart with gladness came;
Me, from Hell's own gate to lift,
And bore me up to praise His name;

Now, His praises ever ring,
Though I've left my earthly home,
Redemption's song with angels sing,
And I'm happy near His throne.

                                        Ivan L. Nelson

Snooze Alert

This section contains some very useful, but perhaps a TINY bit boring, information.

If you need it, you won't be bored reading it – but I put it back here in the back of the book because it is somewhat "textbook-like" in nature.

TYPES OF DEMENTIA

You may hear doctors or other health professionals refer to two main classifications of dementia, under which they categorize all the different types. These two classifications are: *cortical dementia* (referring to the outer layers of the brain, the cortex) and *subcortical dementia* (referring to the sub-cortex, the structures of the brain *below* the cortex). Some doctors find it helpful to use these classifications because they refer to where the initial damage to the brain occurred, but really both kinds affect multiple areas of the brain once they begin to progress, so these two classifications aren't all that important to the patient because each type of dementia has its own set of symptoms and characteristics, as well as prognosis.

All types of dementia are caused by physical changes in the brain. I've included a list of the most common types of dementia and their symptoms. It was taken from the Alzheimer's Association website and it's not exactly the most exciting thing to read, especially if read all at once (z z z z . . .). I'm including it just for your information, so you can read about the type of dementia your loved one may have or find their set of symptoms in one of the types.

I would caution against using the minimal information in this section to "diagnose" someone's symptoms as a certain type. Please see your doctor for that.

Alzheimer's Disease

Most common type of dementia; accounts for an estimated 60 to 80 percent of cases.

Symptoms: Difficulty remembering recent conversations, names or events is often an early clinical symptom; apathy and depression are also often early symptoms. Later symptoms include impaired communication, poor judgment, disorientation, confusion, behavior changes and difficulty speaking, swallowing and walking.

Revised guidelines for diagnosing Alzheimer's were published in 2011 recommending that Alzheimer's be considered a slowly progressive brain disease that begins well before symptoms emerge.

Brain changes: Hallmark abnormalities are deposits of the protein fragment beta-amyloid (plaques) and twisted strands of the protein tau (tangles) as well as evidence of nerve cell damage and death in the brain.

Vascular Dementia

Previously known as multi-infarct or post-stroke dementia, vascular dementia is less common as a sole cause of dementia than

Alzheimer's, accounting for about 10 percent of dementia cases.

Symptoms: Impaired judgment or ability to make decisions, plan or organize is more likely to be the initial symptom, as opposed to the memory loss often associated with the initial symptoms of Alzheimer's. Occurs from blood vessel blockage or damage leading to infarcts (strokes) or bleeding in the brain. The location, number and size of the brain injury determines how the individual's thinking and physical functioning are affected.

Brain changes: Brain imaging can often detect blood vessel problems implicated in vascular dementia. In the past, evidence for vascular dementia was used to exclude a diagnosis of Alzheimer's disease (and vice versa). That practice is no longer considered consistent with pathologic evidence, which shows that the brain changes of several types of dementia can be present simultaneously. When any two or more types of dementia are present at the same time, the individual is considered to have mixed dementia.

Dementia with Lewy Bodies (DLB)

Symptoms: People with dementia with Lewy bodies often have memory loss and thinking problems common in Alzheimer's, but are more likely than people with Alzheimer's to have initial or early symptoms such as sleep disturbances, well-formed visual hallucinations, and slowness, gait imbalance or other parkinsonian movement features.

Brain changes: Lewy bodies are abnormal aggregations (or clumps) of the protein alpha-synuclein. When they develop in a part of the brain called the cortex, dementia can result. Alpha-synuclein also aggregates in the brains of people with Parkinson's disease, but the aggregates may appear in a pattern that is different from dementia with Lewy bodies.

The brain changes of dementia with Lewy bodies alone can cause dementia, or they can be present at the same time as the brain changes of Alzheimer's disease and/or vascular dementia, with each abnormality contributing to the development of dementia. When this happens, the individual is said to have mixed dementia.

Mixed Dementia

In mixed dementia abnormalities linked to more than one cause of dementia occur simultaneously in the brain. Recent studies suggest that mixed dementia is more common than previously thought.

Brain changes: Characterized by the hallmark abnormalities of more than one cause of dementia —most commonly, Alzheimer's and vascular dementia, but also other types, such as dementia with Lewy bodies.

Parkinson's Disease

As Parkinson's disease progresses, it often results in a progressive dementia similar to dementia with Lewy bodies or Alzheimer's.

Symptoms: Problems with movement are common symptoms of the disease. If dementia develops, symptoms are often similar to dementia with Lewy bodies.

Brain changes: Alpha-synuclein clumps are likely to begin in an area deep in the brain called the substantia nigra. These clumps are thought to cause degeneration of the nerve cells that produce dopamine.

Frontotemporal Dementia

Includes dementias such as behavioral variant FTD (bvFTD), primary progressive aphasia, Pick's disease, corticobasal degeneration and progressive supranuclear palsy.

Symptoms: Typical symptoms include changes in personality and behavior and difficulty with language. Nerve cells in the front and side regions of the brain are especially affected.

Brain changes: No distinguishing microscopic abnormality is linked to all cases. People with FTD generally develop symptoms at a younger age (at about age 60) and survive for fewer years than those with Alzheimer's.

Creutzfeldt-Jakob Disease

CJD is the most common human form of a group of rare, fatal brain disorders affecting people and certain other mammals. Variant CJD ("mad cow disease") occurs in cattle, and has been transmitted to people under certain circumstances.

Symptoms: Rapidly fatal disorder that impairs memory and coordination and causes behavior changes.

Brain changes: Results from misfolded prion protein that causes a "domino effect" in which prion protein throughout the brain mis-folds and thus malfunctions.

Normal Pressure Hydrocephalus

Symptoms: Symptoms include difficulty walking, memory loss and inability to control urination.

Brain changes: Caused by the buildup of fluid in the brain. Can sometimes be corrected with surgical installation of a shunt in the brain to drain excess fluid.

Huntington's Disease

A progressive brain disorder caused by a single defective gene on chromosome 4.

Symptoms: Include abnormal involuntary movements, a severe decline in thinking and reasoning skills, and irritability, depression and other mood changes.

Brain changes: The gene defect causes abnormalities in a brain protein that, over time, lead to worsening symptoms.

Wernicke-Korsakoff Syndrome

Korsakoff syndrome is a chronic memory disorder caused by severe deficiency of thiamine (vitamin B-1). The most common cause is alcohol misuse.

Symptoms: Memory problems may be strikingly severe while other thinking and social skills seem relatively unaffected.

Brain changes: Thiamine helps brain cells produce energy from sugar. When thiamine levels fall too low, brain cells cannot generate enough energy to function properly.

* This listing of Types of Dementia was taken from Alz.org and used by permission

Glossa-Pedia

This section may contain a few terms which are unfamiliar to the reader so definitions and clarifications are provided. A glossary gives just the definition of words, while an encyclopedia offers comprehensive reference material. This reference section is a happy medium between the two. I hope it proves to be useful.

ADVANCE CARE DIRECTIVES:

Legal document specifying what actions should be taken for their health if they were incapacitated and no longer able to make those decisions for themselves. Also known as personal directive, medical directive, advance decision, advance directive, or living will.

APHASIA:

A condition that robs you of the ability to communicate. It can affect your ability to speak, write and understand language, both verbal and written.

It typically occurs suddenly after a stroke or a head injury. But it can also come on gradually from a slow-growing brain tumor or a disease that causes progressive, permanent damage (degenerative). Where and how bad the brain damage is and what caused it determine the degree of disability.

CATATONIC:

Inability to move; either rigidity or extreme laxness of limbs.

CHEYNE-STOKES RESPIRATION:

A type of abnormal breathing characterized by a gradual increase in breathing and then a decrease. This pattern is followed by a period of apnea where breathing temporarily stops. Then the cycle repeats itself.

Causes:

Usually related to heart failure or stroke.

It may also be caused by the following conditions:

- Brain tumors
- Chronic pulmonary edema
- Encephalitis
- High altitude sickness
- Increased intercranial pressure
- Traumatic brain injuries

People who are dying often experience Cheyne Stokes breathing. This is a natural effect of the body's attempt to compensate for changing carbon dioxide levels. While it may be distressing to those who witness it, there's no evidence that Cheyne Stokes is stressful for the person experiencing it.

CHRONIC PULMONARY EDEMA

The build-up of fluid in the spaces outside the blood vessels of the lungs. It is a common complication of heart disorders, and most cases of the condition are associated with heart failure. It can be a chronic condition, or it can develop suddenly and quickly become life threatening.

The life-threatening type of pulmonary edema occurs when a large amount of fluid suddenly shifts from the pulmonary blood vessels into the lung, due to lung problems, heart attack, trauma, or toxic chemicals. It can also be the first sign of coronary heart disease.

CIRCADIAN RHYTHM

Often referred to as the "body clock", the circadian rhythm is a cycle that tells our bodies when to sleep, rise, eat--regulating many physiological processes. This internal body clock is affected by environmental cues, like sunlight and temperature.

DELIRIUM

A serious disturbance in mental abilities that results in confused thinking and reduced awareness of your environment. The start of delirium is usually rapid — within hours or a few days.

Delirium can often be traced to one or more contributing factors, such as a severe or chronic medical illness, changes in your metabolic balance (such as low sodium), medication, infection, surgery, or alcohol or drug withdrawal.

Because symptoms of delirium and dementia can be similar, input from a family member or caregiver may be important for a doctor to make an accurate diagnosis.

DEPRESSION (PSEUDO DEMENTIA)

A mood disorder that causes a persistent feeling of sadness and loss of interest. Also called major depressive disorder or clinical depression, it affects how you feel, think and behave and can lead to a variety of emotional and physical problems. You may have trouble doing normal day-to-day activities, and sometimes you may feel as if life isn't worth living.

More than just a bout of the blues, depression isn't a weakness and you can't simply "snap out" of it. Depression may require long-term treatment. But don't get discouraged. Most people with depression feel better with medication, psychotherapy or both.

DSM

The Diagnostic and Statistical Manual of Mental Disorders. Published by the American Psychiatric Association (APA) and offers a common language and standard criteria for the classification of mental disorders.

ENCEPHALITIS

Inflammation of the brain tissue, is rare, affecting about one in 200,000 people each year in the U.S. When it strikes, it can be very serious, causing personality changes, seizures, weakness, and other symptoms depending on the part of the brain affected.

Children, the elderly, and those with a weak immune system are most vulnerable. The disease is usually caused by one of several viral infections, so it's sometimes referred to as viral encephalitis.

Many people who have encephalitis fully recover. The most appropriate treatment and the patient's chance of recovery depend on the virus involved and the severity of the inflammation.

In acute encephalitis, the infection directly affects the brain cells. In para-infectious encephalitis, the brain and spinal cord become inflamed within one to two weeks of contracting a viral or bacterial infection.

GAS-LIGHTING

A form of manipulation that seeks to sow seeds of doubt in a targeted individual or members of a group, hoping to make targets question their own memory, perception, and sanity. Using persistent denial, misdirection, contradiction, and lying, it attempts to destabilize the target and delegitimize the target's belief.

The term originated from a 1940s American movie plot where a husband uses a gas lantern to search for treasure in his attic. When the wife comments about seeing a continual flickering of lights, he tries to convince her through repeated lies and manipulation of circumstances, that she is going insane and imagining things.

HOSPICE CARE

End-of-life care. A team of health care professionals and volunteers provides it. They give medical, psychological, and spiritual support. The goal of the care is to help people who are dying have peace, comfort, and dignity. The caregivers try to control pain and other symptoms so a person can remain as alert and comfortable as possible. Hospice programs also provide services to support a patient's family.

NEUROPSYCHIATRIC SYMPTOMS

Quite common in dementia. These symptoms include agitation, aggression, delusions, hallucinations, wandering, depression, apathy, disinhibition, and sleep disturbances.

NORMAL PRESSURE HYDROCEPHALUS

(NPH), also termed Hakim's syndrome and symptomatic hydrocephalus, is a type of brain malfunction caused by expansion of the lateral cerebral ventricles and distortion of the fibers in the corona radiata. Its typical symptoms are urinary incontinence, dementia, and gait disturbance.

PALLIATIVE CARE

Treatment of the discomfort, symptoms, and stress of serious illness. It provides relief from distressing symptoms including:

- Pain
- Shortness of breath
- Fatigue

- Constipation
- Nausea
- Loss of appetite
- Problems with sleep

It can also help you deal with the side effects of the medical treatments you're receiving.

Hospice care, care at the end of life, always includes palliative care. But you may receive palliative care at any stage of an illness. The goal is to make you comfortable and improve your quality of life.

SLEEP DEFICIT

Sleep deprivation is a condition that occurs if you don't get enough sleep. Sleep deficiency is a broader concept. It occurs if you have one or more of the following:

- You don't get enough sleep (sleep deprivation)
- You sleep at the wrong time of day (that is, you're out of sync with your body's natural clock)

- You don't sleep well or get all of the different types of sleep that your body needs
- You have a sleep disorder that prevents you from getting enough sleep or causes poor quality sleep

Sleeping is a basic human need, like eating, drinking, and breathing. Like these other needs, sleeping is a vital part of the foundation for good health and well-being throughout your lifetime.

Sleep deficiency can lead to physical and mental health problems, injuries, loss of productivity, and even a greater risk of death.

Simply put, *getting enough sleep, and getting the right kind of sleep at the right times is crucial for healthy brain function and emotional well-being.*

SUBDURAL HEMATOMA

A collection of blood outside the brain. Subdural hematomas are usually caused by severe head injuries. The bleeding and increased pressure on the brain from a subdural hematoma can be life-threatening.

Charts

The following charts and forms are ones we are currently using in caring for my friend, Lynn. They have been resized for inclusion here to show their function. You can simply copy and enlarge them, or you can download the full-size version from the website, wittywordsmith.com..

If you need editable versions you can request the MS Word format for customizing to your particular use by emailing me at Judy@Wittywordsmith.com.

Caregiver's Info Sheet
For use with caregiving teams

Caregiver's Name _____

Phone _____

Cell phone _____ Do you text? _____

Email _____

The white boxes indicate time slots that currently need to be filled.

The goal of this caregiving team is to provide Lynn with assistance in maintaining her health and safety.

Keeping her DIET, MEDICATIONS, ACTIVITIES, and REST schedules as consistent as possible will help to extend the time she is able to stay in her own home comfortably.

Please put an X in ALL of the time slots you can fill, indicating whether you can do it EVERY week or EVERY OTHER week.

Also please indicate if you are able to be on call as a backup for the acting caregiver in case help or a replacement is needed. Please CIRCLE the days you can be on call or part of the prayer support team and indicate the frequency with an X.

TIME SLOT	SUN	MON	TUES	WED	THUR	FRI	SAT	ON CALL	PRAYER SUPPORT
9AM – 1PM		Weekly __ Bi-Weekly __	Weekly __ Bi-Weekly __	Weekly __ Bi-Weekly __	Weekly __ Bi-Weekly __	Weekly __ Bi-Weekly __	Weekly __ Bi-Weekly __	M T W TH F Weekly __ Bi-Weekly __	M T W TH F Weekly __ Bi-Weekly __
Please arrive at 9:00am									
1PM – 5PM		Weekly __ Bi-Weekly __	Weekly __ Bi-Weekly __	Weekly __ Bi-Weekly __	Weekly __ Bi-Weekly __	Weekly __ Bi-Weekly __	Weekly __ Bi-Weekly __	M T W TH F Weekly __ Bi-Weekly __	M T W TH F Weekly __ Bi-Weekly __
Please arrive at 12:45pm									
Notes or Questions:									

Thank you for making yourself available to help care for Lynn.

And let us not be weary in well doing: for in due season we shall reap, if we faint not. As we have therefore opportunity, let us do good unto all [men], especially unto them who are of the household of faith.
Galatians 6:9, 10

Home Safety Checklist

Medications:
Safe Use & Storage

- **Keep an updated list of all medications.** Include prescription drugs, as well as over-the counter medications and natural, herbal, or vitamin supplements. Keep this list updated to share with your physician and/or pharmacist.

- **Keep all medications out of reach** of children or anyone who might misuse them. This is especially true of liquid medications that could be mistaken for water or other drinks.

- **Do not mix different medications** together in the same container. This causes difficulty in identifying them during an emergency. Store all medications in their original container. *

- **Always be sure** to take (or administer) medications in an area where good lighting exists to prevent misreading the label.

- **Store medications in a cool, dry place**. Kitchens and bathrooms often have heat and moisture generated which can affect medications. Store all medications together in ONE DESIGNATED LOCATION.

- **Store medications needing refrigeration** in an area of the refrigerator that will not freeze. Make sure they are kept separate from other foods by placing them in a box or tray to visually set them apart and keep them from falling over.

- **Do not share medications** with others which are prescribed to you.

- **DISCARD medications when:**
    - They have been discontinued by your doctor
    - They have expired
    - There is no label on the container

- **WHEN DISCARDING MEDICATIONS**, be sure to throw them out in a way that children or animals will not get to them.

- **When your physician prescribes a new medication,** do the following:
    - Understand the risks and benefits of the medication
    - Understand HOW and HOW OFTEN to check for side effects

* **USE CAUTION** when using daily meds dispensers. Two different medications that are similar in appearance can be mixed up and given at the wrong times. ALWAYS make a clear distinction between similar medications by keeping them separate.

Caregiver Self-Assessment
(FRONT)

Caregiver Self-Assessment

Directions: Caregivers are often so busy caring for a loved one that they tend to neglect their own well-being. This checklist is intended to identify how well you are managing the stress in caring for a loved one. For each question below, circle the number that most appropriately reflects how you are feeling. Add up the points to come up with a total score.

How often have I lately . . .	Please Rate 1-Never, 3=Sometimes, 5=Always (Circle One)
Had trouble staying focused on what I was doing?	1 2 3 4 5
Had difficulty making decisions?	1 2 3 4 5
Felt that I can't leave my relative alone?	1 2 3 4 5
Felt overwhelmed with managing multiple demands (family, work, caregiving)?	1 2 3 4 5
Felt resentful?	1 2 3 4 5
Felt helpless?	1 2 3 4 5
Felt useless?	1 2 3 4 5
Felt lonely?	1 2 3 4 5
Felt weary or tired?	1 2 3 4 5
Felt numb or drained of any feeling?	1 2 3 4 5
Felt anxious?	1 2 3 4 5
Had a crying spell?	1 2 3 4 5
Been physically exhausted?	1 2 3 4 5
Been edgy or irritable?	1 2 3 4 5
Felt ill (headaches, stomach problems, back pain, or common cold)?	1 2 3 4 5
Lost or had poor sleep?	1 2 3 4 5
Either overeaten or had a poor appetite?	1 2 3 4 5
Been upset that my relative has changed so much from his/her former self?	1 2 3 4 5
Additional Questions	
On a scale of 1 to 5, with 1 being "not stressful" to 5 being "extremely stressful," please rate your current level of stress.	1 2 3 4 5
On a scale of 1 to 5, with 1 being "very healthy" to 5 being "very ill," please rate your current health compared to what it was last year.	1 2 3 4 5

Caregiver Self-Assessment
(BACK)

Total Score:

If your score is under 20, you are likely managing the multiple layers of caregiver demands fairly well.

If your score is 21 to 60, you may want to think about some of the suggestions listed below.

If your score is over 60, the stress of caregiving is starting to affect you.

If your score is 80 or above, you are likely feeling burned out.

Having a prolonged level of high stress can cause physical and emotional problems; but you are not alone. This is common and there are many things you can do to better manage your stress and improve your well-being and health.

Consider the following suggestions to improve how you cope with stress and improve your well-being:

• Take care of your health. See your physician for a check-up. Try to improve your diet. Get enough sleep. Exercise.

• Get some relief from your caregiving duties, either from your family or community resources. Spouse, children, sibling, aunts, uncles and other family members, or friends and neighbors could all help with household tasks, driving, managing the finances, and finding services you need. A geriatric care manager, home health aide, homemaker, or other community volunteer could also help. Respite care allows you to take a break for a few hours, a day, or even a weekend.

• Seek support. Join a support group or talk with friends, family, counselor, or pastor about how you feel.

• Take time out for yourself. This includes socializing with friends, getting a massage, reading, meditating, praying, listening to music, or walking - anything that helps you feel calm or more relaxed.

• Give yourself a break. Prioritize what needs to get done; but also set limits and learn to say "no" when asked to take on new tasks. Recognize and deal with negative feelings, such as anger and guilt, which may include confronting and resolving issues with relatives.

Focus on all the good you do for yourself and your family.

Daily Log
(FRONT)

Daily Care Log   DATES: _____

Caregiver, please initial the box next to each item done under the appropriate day & add 1 or 2 sentences of observations on the back.
(Example: We did___ activity or, - She had trouble with... or - she did well with...)

Note: every item is not done every day.

	SUN	MON	TUE	WED	THUR	FRI	SAT
MORNING CARE							
Toileting							
Shower							
Shampoo							
Shaving							
Oral care							
Get dressed							
Breakfast							
Morning meds							
Wound care							
Skin care							
Nail Care							
Other							
AFTERNOON CARE							
Lunch							
Liquids							
Snack							
Exercises							
EVENING CARE							
Dinner							
Dress for bed							
Night meds							
Other							

Daily Log
(BACK)

Daily Notes:

Morning	Afternoon	Evening	
Sunday			
Monday			
Tuesday			
Wednesday			
Thursday			
Friday			
Saturday			

Emergency Medical Information Form
(FRONT)

Emergency Medical Information

CONTAINS CONFIDENTIAL INFORMATION – KEEP IN A SECURE PLACE

Name _____ Address _____

City _____ ST _____ Zip _____ Home Phone _____

Work Phone _____ Cell Phone _____ Email _____

Date of Birth _____ SSN _____ Blood Type _____

Prior Transfusion Reaction (Describe) _____

_____

Please Check all that apply:

Contact lenses ____ Dentures ____ Diabetic ____ Epileptic ____ Metal in body____

Additional Information: _____

Allergies to medications? _____

List all medical conditions: _____

_____

_____

List Dietary Restrictions: _____

List all surgeries and hospitalizations:

Year	Surgery Performed/Reason for Hospitalization	Location

Medicare Beneficiary? Yes __ No __ Medicare Part D? Yes __ No __ Medicare # _____

Supplementary/Insurance Company _____ Phone _____

Group # _____ Policy # _____ Attach Copy of Cards

Preferred Hospital: _____

Primary Physician and/or medical treatment facility:

Physician's Name _____ Phone _____

Emergency Medical Information Form
(BACK)

———————————

Additional physicians/specialists:

Physician's Name _____ Phone _____ Specialty: _____

Physician's Name _____ Phone _____ Specialty: _____

Physician's Name _____ Phone _____ Specialty: _____

Case Manager or Social Worker Information:

Name _____ Agency _____ Agency Phone # _____

Next of kin or person to be notified in an emergency:

Name _____ Relationship _____ Phone _____

Email _____

Name _____ Relationship _____ Phone _____

Email _____

Name _____ Relationship _____ Phone _____

Email _____

Legal Documents: Attach a copy and instructions on where to access originals

Is there a Power of Attorney? Yes ____ No ____

Is there an Advanced Directive or Living Will? Yes ____ No ____

Is there a *Do Not Resuscitate* order? Yes ____ No ____

Health Care Proxy/Power of Attorney Contact Info:

Name _____ Relationship _____ Phone _____

Email _____

Pharmacy phone # _____

Medication List Include prescriptions, over-the-counter, vitamins, homeopathic remedies

Rx Name	Dose	When to take	Reason for taking	Prescribing M.D.

Medications – Safe Use

_____

Medications:
Safe Use & Storage

- **Keep an updated list of all medications.** Include prescription drugs, as well as over-the-counter medications and natural, herbal, or vitamin supplements. Keep this list updated to share with your physician and/or pharmacist.

- **Keep all medications out of reach** of children or anyone who might misuse them. This is especially true of liquid medications that could be mistaken for water or other drinks.

- **Do not mix different medications** together in the same container. This causes difficulty in identifying them during an emergency. Store all medications in their original container. *

- **Always be sure** to take (or administer) medications in an area where good lighting exists to prevent misreading the label.

- **Store medications in a cool, dry place.** Kitchens and bathrooms often have heat and moisture generated which can affect medications. Store all medications together in ONE DESIGNATED LOCATION.

- **Store medications needing refrigeration** in an area of the refrigerator that will not freeze. Make sure they are kept separate from other foods by placing them in a box or tray to visually set them apart and keep them from falling over.

- **Do not share medications** with others which are prescribed to you.

- **DISCARD medications when:**
  - They have been discontinued by your doctor
  - They have expired
  - There is no label on the container

- **WHEN DISCARDING MEDICATIONS**, be sure to throw them out in a way that children or animals will not get to them.

- **When your physician prescribes a new medication,** do the following:
  - Understand the risks and benefits of the medication
  - Understand HOW and HOW OFTEN to check for side effects

* **USE CAUTION** when using daily meds dispensers. Two different medications that are similar in appearance can be mixed up and given at the wrong times. ALWAYS make a clear distinction between similar medications by keeping them separate.

Medications & Supplements

Medications and Supplements Chart

Contact Numbers:

Spouse _____   _____   _____
Doctor _____   _____   _____
Other _____   _____   _____

	Prescribed				Given					
		Frequency			Day	Date				
Med/Supp	Dosage / MG	Times / Day	Times / Week				Med/Supp Given	Dosage Given	Time Given	Caregiver's Initials
Med Name 1	1 tab/500mg	1x/day	Daily	1						
Med Name 2	2 mg	2x/day	3 per	2						
Supp Name	1 tab	3x/day	Daily	3						
				4						
				5						
				6						
				7						
				8						
				9						
				10						
				11						
				12						
				13						
				14						
				15						
				16						
				17						
				18						
				19						
				20						
				21						
				22						
				23						
				24						
				25						
				26						
				27						
				28						
				29						
				30						
				31						

Weekly Care Schedule

_____

Weekly Care Schedule
Important Tasks and Their Approximate Time

Dates: _____

	SUN	MON	TUE	WED	THUR	FRI	SAT
7:00 AM							
8:00							
9:00							
10:00							
11:00							
12:00 PM							
1:00 PM							
2:00							
3:00							
4:00							
5:00							
6:00							
7:00							
8:00							
9:00							
10:00							
11:00							
12:00 Midnight							
1:00 AM							
2:00							
3:00							
4:00							
5:00							
6:00							

Notes:

Resources

It would be next to impossible to list every source I've ever read or gained knowledge from in my studies of dementia and caregiving, but the following list contains some of the more interesting ones for me. I hope you find them to be useful.

1. http://www.agingcare.com
2. http://www.alz.org
3. Elder Care Locator Program:
    http://www.eldercare.gov/Eldercare.NET/Public/Index.aspx
4. http://www.helpforalzheimersfamilies.com/alzheimers-dementia-care-services/
5. 2011 Alzheimer's Disease Facts and Figures, Alzheimer's & Dementia, Volume 7, Issue 2, Alzheimer's Association, 2011, 12-5-2011
6. http://www.brain.northwestern.edu/research/brain/index.html
7. Cognitive Neurology and Alzheimer's Disease Center Newsletter, Northwestern University, Memory, Dementia and AD, 2005, 12-5-2011,
8. Diagnostic and Statistical Manual of Mental Disorders, Fifth Edition (DSM-5)
9. http://www.healthline.com/health/alzheimers-disease/what-it-takes-to-be-a-caregiver
10. JAMA. 2004 Dec 15;292(23):2901-8, Mixed dementia: emerging concepts and therapeutic implications, Langa KM, Foster NL, Larson EB
    https://www.ncbi.nlm.nih.gov/pubmed/15598922

11. The King James Bible
12. http://www.mayoclinic.org/diseases-conditions/depression/home/ovc-20321449
13. https://medlineplus.gov/ency/article/007428.htm
14. National Institute of Neurological Disorders and Stroke Newsletter, NINDS Normal Pressure Hydrocephalus
15. http://neuro.hms.harvard.edu/harvard-mahoney-neuroscience-institute
16. https://www.psychologytoday.com/basics/circadian-rhythm
17. VA Caregiver Support: https://www.caregiver.va.gov/index.asp
18. Warden V, Hurley AC, Volicer L. Development and psychometric evaluation of the pain assessment in advanced dementia (PAINAD) scale.
19. Warrior Navigation and Assistance Program: https://www.humanamilitary.com/beneficiary/plans-and-programs/wnap/
20. http://www.webmd.com/balance/guide/causes-of-stress#1
21. Yale Journal of Biology and Medicine, What do About Normal Pressure Hydrocephalus and When Did They Know It? https://www.ncbi.nlm.nih.gov/pmc/articles/PMC2442723/